THE POLITICS OF ENDING HOMELESSNESS

Susan Yeich

UNIVERSITY
PRESS OF
AMERICA

Lanham • New York • London

Copyright © 1994 by
University Press of America®, Inc.
4720 Boston Way
Lanham, Maryland 20706

3 Henrietta Street
London WC2E 8LU England

Library of Congress Cataloging-in-Publication Data

Yeich, Susan.
The politics of ending homelessness / by Susan Yeich.
p.   cm.
Includes bibliographical references and index.
1. Homelessness – Political aspects – United States.
2. Homelessness – Political aspects – Michigan – Lansing.
3. Homelessness – Government policy – United States.
4. Homelessness – Government Policy – Michigan – Lansing.
5. United States – Social policy.   6. Housing policy – United States.
7. United States – Economic conditions.   I. Title.
HV4505.Y45   1993   362.5'0973—dc20   93-38163 CIP

ISBN 0–8191–9366–6 (cloth : alk. paper)

™ The paper used in this publication meets the minimum requirements of
American National Standard for Information Sciences—Permanence
of Paper for Printed Library Materials, ANSI Z39.48–1984.

Contents

Preface   v

Chapter 1: Introduction   1

Chapter 2: Understanding Homelessness   5

Prevalence of Homelessness   5
Characteristics of the Population   6
Structural Causes of Homelessness   7
  Economic Trends   8
    Changing Employment Opportunities   11
    Structural Economic Change *vs.* Economic Growth   13
  Housing Market Trends   14
    The Gentrification Process   15
    Effects of Gentrification   16
  Political Trends   17
    Less Regulation of Business   18
    Changes in Tax Policy   20
    Conservative Financing   21
    Limited Government   22
      Funding Reductions for Housing   23
      Funding Reductions for Income Support   24
      Funding Reductions by State Governments   24
  Conclusion   25
Government's Response to Homelessness   26
Note   28

Chapter 3: The Homeless and Poor People's Movement   29

The Potential for an Emerging Movement   30
  Structural Sources of Protest   31
  Present Structural Conditions   33
    Economic Pressures   33
      Potential Changes in Government Policy   34
    Breakdown in Regulatory Capacity   44
    Transformation of Consciousness   46
    Changes in Electoral Patterns   49
  Conclusion   50
Potential Forms of the Movement   52
  Potential for Developing Coordinated Protest   53
Potential Successes of the Movement   55
Limitations on the Movement's Success   60
Notes   62

Chapter 4: Protest as the Means to End Homelessness   63

The Role of Outsiders in the Movement   65
  The Concept of Empowerment   68
    Principles for Fostering Empowerment   69
    Supporting the Mobilization of Homeless and Poor People   71
  Conclusion   77

Appendix   79

Bibliography   81

Index   93

Preface

Like many people working in the area of homelessness, I have grown frustrated by the lack of progress to bring an end to this problem. There is a great deal of consensus among professionals in the field about what needs to be done in practical terms to solve homelessness--including restoring the low-cost housing supply, providing livable wage jobs, and raising benefit levels. The barrier arises when attempting to get policy-makers to create the changes.

It was my frustration over this issue which led me to explore in more detail the political nature of homelessness and poverty. The more I considered the politics of the issue, the clearer it became to me that homelessness and poverty were like any other form of oppression. Policy-makers would never willingly create the changes necessary to end the problem because doing so would undermine the interests of their more powerful constituencies. Justice could not be achieved, therefore, by simply appealing to policy-makers to do the right thing, but would have to be forced by an uprising of the oppressed group.

Arriving at this political understanding of homelessness had obvious consequences for my personal work in the area. I came to question the usefulness of top-down approaches to creating progressive social change, and began to see grassroots organizing as the most effective approach. Along with this came my questioning of the roles that professionals should be playing in the struggle to end homelessness. I came to believe that we as "outsiders" can best serve the cause by supporting homeless and low-income people as leaders in the movement for change.

At the time of these personal discoveries, I was in a doctoral program that was based primarily on the top-down philosophy. I decided to remain in the program only if I could incorporate these new insights into my work. Just weeks after this decision, I learned of Unions of the Homeless, which are grassroots organizations comprised of homeless and low-income people working toward a political solution to homelessness. I became involved in the movement, and my experiences with it have confirmed time and time again that homeless and poor people are the appropriate and necessary leaders in the movement to end homelessness.

This book is an outgrowth of my involvement with the Union of the Homeless movement, specifically with the Lansing Area Homeless Person's Union in Lansing, Michigan. It was truly an honor and a pleasure to be a part of these struggles for justice. Because I have grown and learned so much through my involvement with the union movement, union members deserve much credit for this book. While I have had the privilege of working with hundreds of union members, a very special gratitude is extended to the following people with whom I formed especially close relationships: Felida Smith, Gwen Sandy, Edward Thurman, Trina Smith, Brenda Brown, Charles Aikens, and Mark Jones. I also thank other national and statewide leaders of the movement who have contributed to this book, including Leona Smith, Marian Kramer, Diane Bernard, and Wayne Pippin.

Gratitude is also extended to the following individuals for their contribution to the project which led to the writing of this book: Ralph Levine, Deb Bybee, Bill Ewens, and Ellen Strommen.

Finally, a special thanks goes out to Karin Uhlich, who made enormous contributions. Karin offered unlimited advise and suggestions, and provided me with much support and encouragement. Karin's own involvement with the union movement over the past several years, as well as her passion about poverty and justice, made her comments and advise especially helpful.

If we are to move forward in our struggle against homelessness, we must approach the problem as the political issue it is and come to support homeless and low-income people in their rightful role as leaders in the movement. This book was written in the hopes of raising awareness about the politics of the issue and generating support for the growing Homeless and Poor People's Movement.

Chapter 1

Introduction

Since the re-emergence of homelessness as a widespread social problem in the early 1980's, virtually no meaningful action has been taken to solve the problem. Many policy-makers have tried to disregard the problem by attributing blame to its victims. For example, many have claimed people are homeless due to mental illness or substance abuse, or even personal choice. Such attempts to "pathologize" homelessness have offered these policy-makers a convenient justification for inaction. While not all policy-makers have resorted to victim-blaming tactics, very few have been willing to support progressive measures to significantly alleviate homelessness. The legislation that has been passed does not even come close to combating the structural conditions which are giving rise to the problem.

Homelessness can be most accurately understood as one symptom of changing social conditions in our country. Massive changes occurring in the economy and political system have worked to transform our society and create growing inequality. In today's society, the gap between the rich and poor has substantially widened, and many among the poor can no longer afford housing. The fact that the causes of homelessness can be traced to changes in the structure of our society attests to the political nature of the issue, and reveals that homelessness is not a problem that can be blamed on its victims, but on an unequal and unjust society.

Few policy-makers can claim to be unaware of the political nature of homelessness. There has been an abundance of research which has outlined the social structural causes of the problem. In addition, many professional advocacy organizations have been working for years to disseminate this information and persuade policy-makers to take action. Policy-makers as a group have deliberately chosen to serve the interests of more powerful constituencies at the expense of the poor.

Many people undoubtedly attribute this inaction to the conservative nature of the past 12 years, and perhaps expect that Clinton and other new policy-makers will be more receptive to the interests of the poor and that progressive change will become a reality. Such hopes are likely to be violated. As this book discusses at length, Clinton's moderate political background, as well as the reality of the U.S. political system, will work against the implementation of sweeping progressive policies. Perhaps the most that the Clinton administration can be expected to offer is some minor alleviation of hardship for some groups, particularly for the middle classes (or those who have recently fallen from the middle classes) and impoverished children.

History has shown that high-ranking policy-makers do not willingly bestow rights and privileges on impoverished and other oppressed groups. They tend instead to protect the interests of more powerful constituencies. In order for oppressed groups to win concessions from political elites, they must threaten societal stability through protest. Even such past progressive presidents as Kennedy and Roosevelt did not willingly grant concessions to oppressed groups, but were forced to do so by uprisings of oppressed people.

Given this reality of power dynamics within the U.S. political system, it is likely that a resolution to the homelessness problem will require a protest movement of homeless and poor people. There are signs that the potential for a widespread movement may be growing. The rebellion in Los Angeles and other cities in spring of 1992 is one very visible and dramatic demonstration of growing discontent and protest. Other more organized forms of protest have also occurred. Unions of the Homeless, Welfare Rights Unions, and Up and Out of Poverty Now chapters, have arisen in the past decade across the country. These are grassroots organizations comprised of homeless and other low-income people. These groups may constitute the beginnings of a widespread Homeless and Poor People's Movement-- one which may continue to grow and strengthen throughout the 1990's unless serious steps are taken to address the growing problem of economic oppression and disparity.

While it is impossible to predict such an extraordinary and rare phenomenon as a social movement, current conditions appear conducive for the emergence of widespread protest. People have had their expectations about economic security and survival violated due to massive economic changes which are transforming our society. In addition, the ability of social institutions to regulate the lives of many individuals appears to have considerably weakened in recent years. These are two factors thought to encourage the emergence of protest movements among impoverished people (Piven & Cloward, 1977). Given what is known about Clinton's policy intentions--as well as the limitations on him even if he wanted to implement sweeping progressive policies--it appears unlikely that the new administration will do much to lessen the likelihood of protest.

My purpose in writing this book was to highlight the political nature of homelessness--in particular, the political nature of ending the problem. While much effort to solve the problem is currently being made by professional advocacy organizations, advocacy alone is not enough to bring a resolution to the problem. A strategy is needed for pressuring policy-makers to represent the interests of people in poverty. While there are uncertainties associated with the development of a widespread Homeless and Poor People's Movement, a movement is the best, and perhaps the only, hope for significantly alleviating the homelessness problem.

This book is based in part on my personal experiences with the Homeless Union movement. For three years, I worked with a Homeless Person's Union in Lansing, Michigan. I also had the privilege of working with members of the Detroit/Wayne County Union of the Homeless, as well as representatives from the national union headquarters in Philadelphia. My experiences with this movement have only confirmed my belief that homeless and low-income people are the appropriate and necessary leaders in the movement to end homelessness.

This message is certain to be unpopular with many professionals working in the area of homelessness and poverty. It calls into question the whole notion of the "expert" and the appropriateness of the roles that we as outsiders have been playing. Many professionals, along with many in the general public, tend to believe in top-down strategies for creating progressive change. This book challenges the legitimacy of this approach as a useful means for dealing with homelessness and poverty, as well as many other social problems.

As a former adherer to the top-down philosophy, I understand its allure. But if we are to move forward in our fight against homelessness, we must begin challenging our assumptions about creating change and about our appropriate roles in the struggles.

The remainder of this book discusses these issues in detail. The following chapter provides an in-depth analysis of the causes of homelessness. The analysis reveals that homelessness is the product of massive changes which have occurred in the economy, housing market, and political system. By outlining the structural causes of homelessness and how the problem has been minimized through victim-blaming accounts, this chapter sets a foundation for understanding the political nature of homelessness and poverty.

Chapter Three provides some background on the work of Unions of the Homeless, Welfare Rights Unions, and Up and Out of Poverty Now, and discusses the potential for the further development of a protest movement. Based on the work of social movement theorists, a case is made that conditions appear conducive for a widespread movement to occur. A comprehensive analysis of these current conditions is given, and possible forms of protest and potentials for success are described.

Chapter Four discusses the politics of bringing an end to homelessness. Portraying homelessness and poverty as political issues of power and oppression, it is argued that a protest movement will probably be necessary to bring an end to the problem. Based on this analysis, the inherent limitations of professionals and other "outsiders" in bringing an end to homelessness is discussed. It is suggested that the most meaningful action that outsiders can take is to find ways to support and encourage the mobilization of people in poverty.

Chapter 2

Understanding Homelessness

Understanding homelessness requires some background on the prevalence of the problem and general characteristics of the homeless population, but most importantly it requires an awareness of the structural conditions giving rise to the problem. After giving some general background information, this chapter provides an in-depth examination of the structural causes of homelessness. Following this, government's response to homelessness is discussed. By describing the structural nature of homelessness, as well as government's attempts to minimize the problem, this chapter demonstrates that homelessness is not an issue of deviance and pathology, but a political issue of injustice and oppression.

Prevalence of Homelessness

Homelessness re-emerged as a widespread social problem in the early 1980's. At no time since the Great Depression of the 1930's has the number of homeless people been as large as it is today (Hopper, Susser & Conover, 1985). Estimates of the number of homeless people range from a low of 230,000 arrived at by the U.S. Bureau of the Census in 1990 (Toro & Warren, 1991) to a high of at least 3 million (Barak, 1991). The low estimate found by the census has been sharply criticized for failing to count large portions of the homeless population. All estimates provided by the federal government in fact have tended to be on the low end of the continuum. The political implications involved in estimating the extent of homelessness may account for these low figures.

Regardless of the political implications involved, estimating the number of homeless people is obviously a very difficult task, making it hard to determine which estimates are most accurate. And perhaps even more important than the actual current number is the fact that the number is steadily increasing. Some studies have found that the population is increasing at a rate of 20 to 25% annually (National Coalition for the Homeless, 1988; Reyes & Waxman, 1989). A 1988 congressionally-funded study by the Neighborhood Reinvestment Corporation has estimated that by the end of the century there could be as many as 19 million homeless people in the U.S., unless immediate action is taken to preserve and expand the supply of affordable housing (Barak, 1991).

Characteristics of the Population

While debate continues over estimating the prevalence of the problem, there is consensus among researchers that demographic characteristics of the homeless population have changed significantly from populations of past eras. Compared to previous eras, researchers have found today's homeless population to be younger (Freeman & Hall, 1987; Redburn & Buss, 1987; Wright & Lam, 1987), to have a higher proportion of women (Stoner, 1983; Wright & Lam, 1987), to have an overrepresentation of minorities (Barak, 1991; First, Roth & Arewa, 1988; Freeman & Hall, 1987; Wright & Lam, 1987), to have higher levels of formal education (Wright & Lam, 1987), and to have a higher proportion of families (National Coalition for the Homeless, 1988; Wright & Lam, 1987).

Families comprise approximately 30% of the homeless population and have been found to be the fastest growing segment of the population (National Coalition for the Homeless, 1988; Reyes & Waxman, 1989). In a survey of 29 major cities, the U.S. Conference of Mayors estimated that children and their parents comprised an average of 32% of the homeless population in 1992. They estimated that the remainder of the population was comprised of single men (55%), single women (11%), and unaccompanied youth (2%). The racial composition of the population was estimated to be 52% African American, 33% Anglo, 11% Latino American, 3% Native American, and 1% Asian American. In addition, they estimated that 17% were employed on a full- or part-time basis, and that 18% were veterans (Waxman & Frye, 1992).

Structural Causes of Homelessness

An awareness of the structural conditions giving rise to homelessness is critical in understanding the homelessness problem. Homelessness can be most accurately understood as one symptom of changing social conditions in the U.S. Changes in society occurring over the past two or three decades have dramatically altered the social class structure and given rise to the current epidemic of homelessness. Trends that began in the 1960's and intensified in the 1980's, have resulted in a dramatic redistribution of wealth which has considerably widened the gap between the rich and poor.

To illustrate these changes, consider the following information compiled by the Center on Budget and Policy Priorities. Using Congressional Budget Office data, they examined changes in income for various economic classes from 1980 to 1990. They found that income gaps among the classes increased substantially over this decade, with wealthy classes reaping large income gains, middle class incomes stagnating, and low income classes falling further behind. Specifically, they found the following (regarding the after-tax income of these groups):

* income of the poorest fifth of households fell 5%
* income of the middle fifth grew less than 3%
* income of the top fifth grew 33%
* income of the richest 1 percent grew 87%.

By 1990, the after-tax income of the richest 1 percent nearly matched that of the bottom 40 percent (Greenstein & Barancik, 1990). From 1980 to 1989, the total wages of people who earned less than $50,000 per year--85% of all citizens--increased an average of only 2% per year. By contrast, the total wages of all millionaires rose 243% per year (Barlett & Steele, 1992). By the end of the decade, .5% of the population owned 45% of the nation's financial assets, excluding the value of private homes. Another 9.5% of the population--the affluent--owned 38% of the assets, while 90% of the population owned only 17% (Barak, 1991).

The number of very rich people also grew dramatically over the decade. The number of people reporting incomes of more than a half-million dollars soared from 16,881 to 183,240--an increase of 985%. That increase represents the largest in this century, even exceeding the 854% jump from 1920 to 1929 (Barlett & Steele, 1992). The number of millionaires and billionaires also grew dramatically. The number of millionaires has burgeoned in recent years--increasing from 180,000 in 1972 to 1.3 million in 1988. The number of billionaires has grown from just a handful in 1981, to 26 in 1986, to 52 in 1988 (Phillips, 1992).

By contrast, the Census Bureau reported that 14.2% of all Americans lived in poverty in 1991, up from 11.7% in 1979. The rise in the poverty rate for children was even more dramatic, increasing from 16.4% in 1979 to 21.8% in 1991. The poverty rate for working families with children also increased--by almost 25% between 1980 and 1991 (Greenstein & Jaeger, 1992). According to census data, in 1991 the number of poor people in the country reached its highest level in more than 20 years, with 35.7 million citizens living in poverty. Poverty continues to affect minorities disproportionately. In 1991, the poverty rate was 32.7% for African Americans, 28.7% for Latino Americans, and 11.3% for Anglos (Greenstein & Jaeger, 1992).

The following sections discuss how trends in the economy, housing market, and political system have transformed the social structure and resulted in this dramatic redistribution of wealth and the corresponding epidemic of homelessness. While trends in these three areas are presented separately, they are in fact integrally related.

Economic Trends

At the core of the changing social class structure are economic trends which have resulted in a dramatic shift in income distribution. There is an increasing concentration of jobs at the extremes of the country's range of earnings (Harrison & Bluestone, 1990; Hopper, et al., 1985; Kuttner, 1983; Winpisinger, 1985). In previous decades, the country had few jobs at the extremes and many in the middle; in today's economy, many of the middle positions are disappearing. Because of the polarization of job earnings, the U.S. is losing its middle class, and there is a corresponding widening gap between rich and poor (Kuttner, 1983; Reich, 1991).

At the root of these changes in job opportunities is the massive economic transformation which has taken place in the past two to three decades. The country has been undergoing a major shift from an industrial base to an information and service base (Adams, 1986; Hopper et al., 1985; Kuttner, 1983; Loewenstein, 1985; Staudohar & Brown, 1987). While the effects of this transformation began to be felt in the mid-1970's, the effects were intensified throughout the 1980's (Loewenstein, 1985).

Advances in technology have played a major role in spurring this transformation. Innovations in such fields as computers and robotics have allowed companies to restructure their production process and develop more efficient, automated production techniques. Such innovations have eliminated the need for many manufacturing jobs (Harrington, 1984; Hopper et al., 1985; Kuttner, 1983; Reich, 1991; Samuel, 1985; Staudohar & Brown, 1987; Winpisinger, 1985).

Advances in technology have also spurred the development of another trend which has further eroded the U.S. industrial base. Technological innovations in transportation and communications have resulted in significantly greater capital mobility, allowing corporations to transfer production sites from one country or region to another (Bluestone, 1987; Bluestone & Harrison, 1982; Kuttner, 1983; Thelwell, 1985). While corporate flight has always been a tactic used by management to gain power over labor (Bluestone & Harrison, 1982), in the 1960's and 1970's a significant trend toward production on an international scale emerged (Bluestone & Harrison, 1982; Fuentes & Ehrenreich, 1983; Harrington, 1984; Kuttner, 1983). This trend accelerated in pace during the 1980's. In fact, between 1980 and 1990, U.S. companies increased their investments in foreign countries at a higher rate than in the U.S. By 1990, more than 20% of the output from U.S.-owned corporations was being produced in foreign countries (Reich, 1991).

Corporations began moving production sites to other countries when they were faced with intensifying global competition and a series of organized labor victories over management (Bluestone & Harrison, 1982). Third World countries have often been a favorite relocation site for multinational corporations. Transferring production sites to these countries has allowed multinationals to maximize their profits by exploiting cheap labor, avoiding union demands, reducing taxation, and avoiding environmental and other regulatory restrictions (Fuentes & Ehrenreich, 1983). This trend has led not only to detrimental effects for impoverished people of Third

World countries (Frank, 1972; Fuentes & Ehrenreich, 1983), but also to the displacement of U.S. industrial workers.

The flight of U.S. production sites to Mexico has been one of the more publicized trends in recent years. Ratification of the North American Free Trade Agreement (NAFTA) will encourage even more flight across the border. NAFTA would eliminate existing barriers to the movement of capital and goods within the three North American countries. Labor economists have estimated that 7 to 8 million manufacturing jobs--constituting 7% of the U.S. workforce--may be lost under the agreement (Uchitelle, 1993).

In fact, despite propaganda to the contrary, the sole beneficiaries of current free trade proposals are multinational corporations (Dawkins & Muffett, 1993). For multinationals NAFTA, as well as the global free trade proposals under the General Agreement on Tariffs and Trade (GATT), mean freedom to maximize profits through reduced government regulation. For the rest of us, they mean weakened labor protection laws, environmental regulations, and public health and safety standards (Dawkins & Muffett, 1993). One critic of NAFTA has in fact called it a "corporate bill of rights" (Weintraub, 1993).

The fact that the free trade proposals favor business interests is demonstrated by the overwhelming support of big business for the agreements. NAFTA was backed from the beginning by a coalition of Fortune 500 corporations (Moody, 1992a). Big business in fact played a major role in designing the agreements. The overall strategy for the U.S. in the GATT negotiations was designed by the chief executive officer of American Express, one of the largest multinationals in the world (Dawkins & Muffett, 1993). In addition, advisory committees for the U.S. trade negotiators for both GATT and NAFTA are packed with more than 1,000 representatives from the business world. By comparison, only five environmentalists were asked by the U.S. trade representative for their suggestions on NAFTA (Dawkins & Muffett, 1993). The trade negotiations were so secretive that one of the few sources of information for citizens' groups representing labor and environmental concerns was a leaked copy of the first complete draft of the text of the agreement (Weintraub, 1993).

The effects these free trade agreements may have on encouraging further corporate flight, as well as increasing environmental contamination and reducing consumer safety, depends on the actions taken by the Clinton administration. It appears at this point that the actions will not be sufficient to prevent the adverse effects of the agreements. Clinton is not planning to renegotiate NAFTA, but only to add legislation to aid displaced workers and protect the environment--measures described as completely inadequate to significantly impact the agreement (Weintraub, 1993). In addition, Clinton is seeking a rapid conclusion to GATT, indicating that substantial revisions to the proposals are unlikely (Dawkins & Muffett, 1993).

Without substantial revisions, ratification of the agreements will open up virtually unlimited opportunities for multinationals to enhance their power and profits. Under NAFTA, for example, "all enterprises with substantial business activities in a NAFTA country" can buy or invest in any company in North America (Moody, 1992b). In addition, both NAFTA and GATT contain provisions for overturning laws in any country which are deemed "trade restrictive" or "trade distorting." This means that corporations will be granted open access to all markets in the participating countries, regardless of previous national laws which sought to protect labor, public health and safety, and the environment (Dawkins & Muffett, 1993). Corporations, therefore, will have the dual benefit of minimizing production costs through corporate flight tactics, while simultaneously ensuring that products manufactured under such unregulated and exploitative conditions have legal access to all possible markets.

The transformation to the post-"Cold War" era is yet another occurrence which is opening up more opportunities for multinational corporations (Barak, 1991; Harrison & Bluestone, 1990). As Cochburn (1990) put it: "under the sheltering sky of a world market and the open vista of free trade, the task (for multinational corporations) is simply to roam the planet for cheaper labor" (cited in Barak, 1991, p. 176).

Changing Employment Opportunities

The relocation of production sites to other countries, as well as the trend toward automated production, have created a corresponding shift in U.S. job opportunities. Government labor market statistics indicate sharp declines in manufacturing, transportation, and construction employment, and increases in finance, trade, and service employment (Loewenstein, 1985). During the 1950's, 33% of all workers were employed in manufacturing. That figure dropped to 30% in the 1960's and to 20% in the 1980's. By the beginning of the

1990's, the figure was at 17% and falling (Barlett & Steele, 1992). The 500 largest U.S. industrial companies in fact produced no net increase in the number of U.S. jobs between 1975 and 1990, and their share of the civilian work force dropped from 17% to less than 10% during the same period (Reich, 1991).

In just one decade--from 1981 to 1991--a total of 1.8 million manufacturing jobs were lost in the country--a decline of 9% (Barlett & Steele, 1992). Since the mid-1970's, plant closings alone have eliminated more than 900,000 jobs every year (Harris, 1987). It is predicted that only 11% of the work force will be in manufacturing by the year 2000, and only 3% by the year 2030. By contrast, 55% of workers were in information industries in 1984, and 80% are predicted to be by the year 2000 (Feingold, 1984). "In-person service" jobs accounted for about 30% of U.S. jobs in 1990, and their numbers are rapidly growing (Reich, 1991). Retail-trade jobs alone increased 32.5% from the 1970's to the 1980's (Barlett & Steele, 1992).

These changing employment opportunities are dramatically affecting the social class structure. Many jobs offering a middle-class standard of living are disappearing and are being replaced by high-paid, specialized and technical positions on one hand, and low-paid, low-skilled, often part-time positions on the other (Harrison & Bluestone, 1990; Hopper et al., 1985; Kuttner, 1983; Winpisinger, 1985). While the new economic base is generating jobs on both ends of the wage scale, there is a disproportionate number being created on the low end (Harrison & Bluestone, 1990; Kuttner, 1983). Forty-four percent of the new jobs created since 1980 in fact pay poverty-level wages (Marcuse, 1988), and one-half of the jobs in the growing producer services sector are in the next to lowest income class (Hopper, et al., 1985). Retail-trade jobs, for example, pay an average of only $204 per week, compared to an average of $458 per week paid by manufacturing jobs (Barlett & Steele, 1992).

From 1979 to 1989 the proportion of workers paid low wages rose by more than one-third (Jaeger, Shapiro & Greenstein, 1992). U.S. Department of Labor data show that after adjustment for inflation, average hourly wages paid for non-supervisory workers were lower in 1991 than in any year since 1963. Wages fell even during the recovery of the 1980's (Hutchinson, Lav & Greenstein, 1992). According to a study by the Economic Policy Institute, real wages and salaries for all workers fell 10.5% between 1977 and 1989, compared to an increase of 17.8% between 1966 and 1972, and recent data reveal a continuation of this downward trend (Boroughs, Hage,

Collins & Cohen, 1992). While such a pattern of declining wages does not necessarily imply increased inequality, data show that inequality did in fact increase during this period (Harrison & Bluestone, 1990). While inequality fell dramatically from 1963 to the mid- to late 1970's, a pronounced reversal of this trend has occurred since then--what Harrison and Bluestone (1988) have termed the "Great U-Turn."

One explanation for rising inequality is that the power of labor has been severely undermined by structural economic changes. Corporate flight has served not only to displace U.S. industrial workers, but has often been used as a threat to force organized labor to make wage concessions (Bluestone, 1987). And since many jobs in the growing service sector have not yet been unionized (Kuttner, 1983), companies have had virtually complete control over wage levels and benefits for these positions. The proportion of organized labor in the U.S. workforce in fact has declined markedly in recent years. The percent of nonagricultural workers belonging to a union dropped from 35% in 1960 to 17% in 1990. Excluding government employees, the proportion of unionized workers is just over 13%--which is lower than it was in the early 1930's before workers had the legal right to unionize (Reich, 1991).

Structural Economic Change vs. Economic Growth

This changing pattern of job opportunities is an issue distinct from problems of poor economic growth. Enhanced economic growth will not alter this trend toward a polarized wage distribution (Kuttner, 1983). Economic growth may lead to higher employment rates and more profit for the rich, but will not curtail the structural trend which is keeping many people in low-paying jobs. The issue today is not merely how much capital the country has, but how the resources are distributed among social classes.

Recovery from the recession of the early 1990's, therefore, will not bring a return of many high-paying manufacturing jobs. Indeed, while the recession technically ended in April 1991, the recovery has failed to produce a sufficient number of jobs--either high- or low-paying. Three million additional jobs should have been created by this stage in the recovery, compared to previous economic recoveries (Moberg, 1993).

The current recovery in fact appears to be on precarious grounding, and structural economic changes may partially explain this situation.

Increased consumer demand has been matched and actually surpassed by increased productivity, but the rising productivity is due to increased worker output, not to an increase in the number of workers--a situation which has left millions of workers unemployed (Hage & Collins, 1993). In addition, those who are employed have not received the usual wage increases seen during previous recoveries--income growth has risen at less than one-third the average rate of past recoveries (Moberg, 1993).

Because this problem of low wages is arising from structural economic changes, it will likely have long-term consequences for economic growth. With lower incomes, consumers will have less money to spend. Some economists in fact have expressed concern that the impaired spending ability of a growing fraction of the workforce could create problems of insufficient demand (Harrison & Bluestone, 1990).

Current economic problems, therefore, cannot be fully understood without an awareness of the structural economic changes which are transforming the economy. Traditional strategies of stimulating economic growth will not be sufficient to address these problems. Even if the recovery would begin to create additional jobs, many of the positions would continue to be low-paying. The structural nature of current economic problems will ultimately require that the root causes of the problems--which involve the growing inequality among social classes--be addressed.

Housing Market Trends

These structural economic changes are integrally related to the diminishing supply of low-cost housing. Deindustrialization of cities in fact is the primary cause of the low-cost housing shortage (Adams, 1986; Hopper, 1988; Hopper et al., 1985; Marcuse, 1988). Service and information-based cities require a different physical environment than manufacturing-based cities (Adams, 1986; Hopper et al., 1985) and create a demand for high quality housing adjacent to business districts (Marcuse, 1988).

Exploring historical patterns of homelessness and housing reveals how current homelessness is different from that found during other periods. Marcuse (1988) outlined housing conditions present in different historical stages. Four of the periods apply to U.S. development. During the "non-industrial" period, resources were lacking to provide all people with housing, and some people were without homes for this reason. During "early industrialization," migration to cities caused a lack of housing, but efforts were continually made to construct more housing. During "mature industrialization," there was an unstable balance between the number of low-paid workers and unemployed people and the number of housing units available to them. The extent of homelessness was cyclical, therefore, following fluctuations in employment and wages. During "deindustrialization," the dramatic decline of manufacturing jobs, the rise in service jobs, and the heightened international division of labor, have caused gentrification and the displacement of low-income residents.

The current epidemic of homelessness, therefore, has been caused by an economic transformation, not merely a decline in economic growth. It is often assumed that economic growth will help alleviate homelessness. This belief may be a carry-over from the previous period of "mature industrialization." As stated above, the issue today is not economic growth per se, but how the resources are distributed among social classes. With the changing structure of the economy, economic growth can in some ways actually exacerbate the problem of homelessness. Increased economic growth can create greater demand for property, which leads to more gentrification (Freeman & Hall, 1987).

The Gentrification Process

Gentrification can be defined as a process by which people with higher incomes reclaim low-income neighborhoods, resulting in the displacement of existing residents (Hopper, 1988). Gentrification not only involves a "household-driven" process, where individual higher-income households move back into the city, but also a "developer-driven" process, which includes condominium conversion and other revitalization efforts (Beauregard, 1988). Gentrification has typically been viewed as merely a "back to the city" movement by suburbanites. Such a simple explanation does nothing to expose the economic and political causes behind the process. The public and private sectors actually operate together to create gentrification (Kasinitz, 1984; Moore, Sink & Hoban-Moore, 1988).

Two stages are necessary in order for gentrification to occur. First there must be a disinvestment of resources from low-income neighborhoods, which leads to deterioration and makes the area an undesirable place to live. This often serves to persuade current residents to leave and results in lowering property values. Residents who do not choose to leave can be forced out by procedures such as condemning buildings or other legal action. Once property values are sufficiently low, the second stage occurs as developers purchase the property and construct more profitable structures. This second stage is made possible by a reinvestment of resources in the area (Beauregard, 1988).

There are several players in this process. Governments frequently play a role in both the disinvestment process and reinvestment process by first withdrawing services from the areas, then offering tax abatements, low-cost loans, and infrastructure improvements to private developers to build structures to serve higher-income groups (Beauregard, 1988; Hartman, Keating & LeGates, 1982; Hopper et al., 1985; Kasinitz, 1984; Marcuse, 1988). The advantages of gentrification for governments are obvious. Gentrification means rising property tax revenue, more wage and sales tax revenue due to more affluent consumers, and less need for government intervention and expenditure (Beauregard, 1988).

Lending institutions, landlords, and private developers are other players in the gentrification process. Lending institutions and landlords often encourage abandonment of low-cost housing by disinvesting resources from the areas. Lending institutions do this by denying credit to certain areas, a process called "redlining" (Hopper et al., 1985; Wright & Lam, 1987). Landlords often participate in this process by letting housing deteriorate instead of making necessary repairs. Even landlords who would be willing to make repairs are often unable to do so because of "redlining" practices (Hopper et al., 1985). Once the disinvestment process is complete, private developers step in--buying the property for very low prices and making renovations to increase property value (Beauregard, 1988).

Gentrification of low-income neighborhoods is a process created by certain groups who benefit economically and politically from it. The transformation of the economy has made the revitalization of cities desirable for these groups, and their power over other groups in society has made the process feasible.

Effects of Gentrification

The benefits to these powerful groups have resulted in increased hardship for the less powerful. Nationwide, 1.5 to 2 million people experienced involuntary displacement each year during the mid-1970's

(Beauregard, 1988). As of 1986, 2.5 million people were losing their homes each year (Riessman, 1986). The current U.S. housing situation has been described as a nation of housing "haves" and "have-nots" (Apgar, DiPasquale, Cummings & McArdle, 1990). The number of low-income households has increased dramatically, while the number of low-cost housing units has decreased dramatically (Apgar & Brown, 1988; Hopper, 1988; Marcuse, 1988; McChesney, 1990; Shapiro & Greenstein, 1988; Shinn, 1990; Wright & Lam, 1987).

In a recent study of housing conditions in 44 of the 50 largest metropolitan areas, the Center on Budget and Policy Priorities found that there was a substantial shortage of affordable housing. In the typical large metropolitan area, the ratio of low-income renters to low-cost housing units was nearly two to one. In 1970, there were 6.8 million low-cost units and 6.4 million low-income renters--a surplus of 400,000 units. By 1989, the number of low-cost units fell to 5.5 million, while the number of low-income renters grew to 9.6 million, resulting in a shortage of 4.1 million units. One of the primary factors accounting for the diminishing supply of affordable housing has been a steady decline in the number of unsubsidized low-cost units in the private market. Between the mid-1970's and the late 1980's, the number of unsubsidized low-cost units fell 54% in the typical large metropolitan area. The increase in the number of federally-subsidized low-cost units failed to keep pace with the decline, resulting in an overall contraction of the low-cost housing supply (Leonard & Lazere, 1992).

Political Trends

Changes in the political system which began in the late 1960's and culminated in the "Reagan Revolution" of the 1980's, have played a major role in the redistribution of wealth and the corresponding epidemic of homelessness. To some extent, these changes encompass the trends in the economy and housing market already discussed. As Barlett and Steele (1992) described it, the economy operates under the framework of a "government rule book"--a system of rewards and penalties set by Congress and the president that influences business behavior and, in turn, has profound effects on the lives of all individuals within the system. During the 1970's and 1980's, the rule book was dramatically altered to serve the interests of the privileged few at the expense of all others (Barlett & Steele, 1992).

While this "rule book" has lost some of its jurisdiction due to the advent of global capitalism (an issue discussed in detail in the following chapter), there is no question that government policies play a significant role in economic operations and in the distribution of wealth. At a minimum, it can be argued that Reagan and Bush policies worked in conjunction with structural economic changes to greatly intensify the inequitable distribution of wealth and to encourage the gentrification of cities.

This is not the first time in this country's history that changes made in government policies have resulted in a regressive redistribution of wealth. In the past 100 years, there were two other such periods. The first was during the post-Civil War Gilded Age of the late Nineteenth Century, and the second was during the Roaring Twenties in the first part of this century (Phillips, 1992). These wealth redistribution periods did not occur in isolation, but marked the culmination of Republican-dominated eras. Phillips (1992) has described how the early stages of Republican-dominated eras are characterized by broad-based themes of national unity. It is in later stages that policies which result in the redistribution of wealth begin. Phillips has termed these redistribution eras "capitalist heydays," and notes that both previous capitalist heydays were followed by severe economic depressions and societal instability.

Even though Carter was a Democratic president within a Republican-dominated era, the first signs of the emerging capitalist heyday began under his administration in the late 1970's. His administration in fact set a foundation for later conservative agendas through its own policies of economic deregulation, tax-rate reduction for capital gains, and tight-money Federal Reserve Board policies (Phillips, 1992). With the inauguration of Reagan in 1981, the capitalist heyday was fully underway. Similar to other heyday periods, the Reagan administration made sweeping changes in government policies, which included less regulation of business, changes in tax policy, conservative financing, and limited government. As Phillips (1992) has outlined, these four areas of policy changes are major factors in the redistribution of wealth.

Less Regulation of Business

Reduced government regulation of business played a fundamental role in the redistribution of wealth in the 1980's. With the foundation for deregulation set by the Carter administration in 1980, the Reagan administration maintained and intensified deregulation of business, discarding decades worth of regulations and restraints (Barlett & Steele, 1992; Bluestone & Harrison, 1982; Phillips, 1992).

These deregulation policies had disastrous consequences in the 1980's. The new permissive approach to mergers, antitrust enforcement, and new forms of speculative financing, resulted in a surge of hostile takeovers and leveraged buyouts (Phillips, 1992), and this in turn led to an explosion of corporate debt and corporate bankruptcies (Barlett & Steele, 1992). Corporations organizing takeovers went into debt in order to finance acquisitions; corporations targeted for takeovers went into debt trying to resist the maneuvers. During the 1980's, the number of businesses filing bankruptcy petitions increased 155% from the 1970's and 302% from the 1960's-- the largest growth in bankruptcy cases since the Great Depression of the 1930's (Barlett & Steele, 1992). The diversion of capital from productive investment in basic national industries into unproductive speculation, mergers and acquisitions, and foreign investment, has been described as the essential problem with the U.S. economy (Bluestone & Harrison, 1982).

Throughout the 1980's, it became increasingly apparent that wealthy individuals and financial institutions were the beneficiaries of deregulation (Barlett & Steele, 1992; Jonas, 1986; Phillips, 1992). Low- and moderate-income people were actually being hurt by deregulation policies. Deregulation resulted in thousands of firms disappearing and a loss of 200,000 jobs from the trucking and airline industries alone (Barlett & Steele, 1992). The corporate debt explosion and resulting bankruptcies led to the loss of even more jobs. As in all conservative deregulation periods, the power of organized labor was undermined. Three million union workers in airlines, telecommunications, trucking, bus transportation, and other areas, suffered wage cuts (Phillips, 1992).

In addition to loss of jobs and lower wages, moderate- and low-income people will suffer other long-term consequences resulting from deregulation practices. For example, many people believe the Savings and Loan crisis can be traced to deregulation policies which allowed S & L's to invest funds much more freely (Phillips, 1992). For years to come, the economy (and therefore, workers) will suffer from the burden of increased federal debt created by the S & L bailout, and taxpayers will be forced to pay it off, while many of the culprits of the disaster either receive minimal or no prison time and are allowed to keep their immense fortunes.

Changes in Tax Policy

A fundamental component of Reagan economic policy involved changes in federal income taxation. The Reagan administration was successful in passing two pieces of legislation that dramatically altered the existing tax structure: the 1981 Economic Recovery Tax Act and the 1986 Tax Reform Act. While the rhetoric of the time claimed that these new taxation policies would bring relief to the middle classes, it later become apparent that the changes actually hurt middle- and low-income classes, while they helped the wealthy (Barak, 1991; Barlett & Steele, 1992; Phillips, 1992; Reich, 1991).

While the 1981 legislation resulted in some minor cuts in income tax for middle-income groups, changes made in Reagan's second term served to cancel out previous reductions (Phillips, 1992). Rising Social Security tax rates--which reflected an additional component of tax policy changes--were the principal reason for this (Phillips, 1992). These policies placed a disproportionate burden on middle- and low-income people. Social Security tax in fact works like the income tax in reverse--it favors high incomes, rather than low incomes (Reich, 1991). During the 1950's, median-income families paid 1.7% of their income for the entire decade on Social Security taxes. During the 1980's, they paid 7% of their income. Affluent families (representing those with income 10 times the median) paid two-tenths of 1% of their income for Social Security taxes during the 1950's, and still paid less than 1% during the 1980's (Barlett & Steele, 1992).

In order to assess the overall effects of tax policy changes from 1977 to 1987, the Congressional Budget Office calculated the combined impact of all federal taxes--individual income, Social Security, corporate income, and excise--on different income classes. They found that only the richest 10% of families paid lower effective tax rates in 1987, while the bottom 90% of the population actually paid higher rates (Phillips, 1992). Using Congressional Budget Office data in 1990, the Center on Budget and Policy Priorities found that the percentage of income paid in federal taxes by the poorest fifth of households was 16% higher in 1990 than in 1980. The percentage paid by the middle fifth was 1% higher, while the percentage paid by the wealthiest one percent of households was 14% lower (Greenstein & Barancik, 1990).

It is now apparent that the real beneficiaries of the Reagan tax cuts were the very wealthy. Under Reagan, the tax rate for the top personal tax bracket dropped from 70% to 28%, the top rate on capital gains was reduced to 20%, and taxation on unearned income (including rental and interest income) was capped at 50% (Phillips, 1992). Corporate tax rates were also reduced. By 1983, income tax revenue from corporations accounted for only 6.2% of all federal tax receipts, down from 32.1% in 1952 and 12.5% in 1980 (Phillips, 1992).

These tax policy changes have dramatically affected the distribution of wealth in this country, and in turn the extent of homelessness. One other very significant change which was made in the 1986 tax reform, has had perhaps an even more direct effect on homelessness. The 1986 Act removed many tax and investment incentives for real estate developers to build low-cost housing (Dreier, 1987), thus further encouraging the gentrification of cities and contributing to the low-cost housing shortage.

Conservative Financing

The economic and fiscal policies of the Reagan administration were major factors in the redistribution of wealth in the 1980's. Reagan combined a supply-side economic theory--which Budget Director David Stockman admitted was the Republican's latest version of "trickle-down" theory (Phillips, 1992)--with a tight money policy which severely limited the rate of money expansion (Belcher & Singer, 1988; Phillips, 1992; Thelwell, 1985).

Tight money supply is a deflation strategy which makes money buy more, but hurts those who sell products because prices are forced down. Tight money policies favor the financial sector of the economy and owners of financial assets, and promote a Darwinian economic restructuring and redistribution of wealth (Phillips, 1992). These effects became evident by the early 1980's as the percentage of the national income represented by wages and salaries declined, while the percentage represented by interest income soared. The policies produced enormous gains particularly for the richest one percent of U.S. households, who experienced burgeoning after-tax incomes (Phillips, 1992).

While Reagan's conservative fiscal policies benefitted the financial sector and owners of financial assets, they severely damaged other sectors in the economy, including manufacturing, the housing market, and the extractive sector (Phillips, 1992). By 1985, the high-deficit, high-interest-rate policies had strengthened the dollar to such an extent that U.S. manufacturing and agriculture were losing out to foreign competition (Bywater, 1985; Phillips, 1992). The value of the dollar had been pushed up more than 70% against the currencies of major U.S. trading partners--a situation which resulted in further job losses by creating a soaring trade deficit (Bywater, 1985). In order to save these industries, a drastic devaluation of the dollar began. While this new policy helped these industries recover, the flood of money into the system did not help reverse the growing income disparity among social classes. Much of the money flowed into the financial sector--enabling takeovers and mergers, and resulting in a soaring stock market until the crash in 1987 (Phillips, 1992).

While increased debt is a basic characteristic of capitalist heydays, the Reagan Revolution differed from previous heyday periods in that the policies resulted in huge federal government deficits, and the debt strategies not only rearranged assets domestically, but also transferred some to other countries (Phillips, 1992). In addition, while the two previous heyday periods were marked by an increase in the U.S. share of world GNP, the 1980's heyday was marked by a significant decline in the U.S. share. The U.S. percentage of world GNP fell from about 40% in the 1950's to under 30% in the 1970's, and by 1989 economists were predicting that the U.S. share would drop to only 25% in the 1990's (Phillips, 1992). Under the Reagan administration's policies, the focus of business activity was on rearranging financial assets, not on creating actual products. The policies encouraged "money games," such as mergers and acquisitions, as a means for making money, instead of encouraging the production of goods with some actual value (Barlett & Steele, 1992).

The Reagan and Bush administrations' conservative fiscal policies, therefore, resulted not only in increasing economic disparity among social classes, but also in an enormous federal debt and decreased U.S. competitiveness in the global economy. These developments will have serious long-term ramifications for the U.S. economy, and ultimately, for the U.S. workforce. In the end, it will be middle- and low-income people who will suffer the consequences of failed policies which they did not create.

Limited Government

Perhaps the area of policy changes most visibly associated with the redistribution of wealth and the corresponding increase in homelessness is the reallocation of government spending which arose from the Republican philosophy of limited government in domestic affairs. The Reagan administration dramatically altered the pattern of federal funding--making severe cuts in domestic programs and hugh increases in military defense. From 1980 to 1987, spending for human resources decreased from 28% of all federal allocations to only 22%, while spending for defense rose from 23% to 28% (Phillips, 1992). Under the Reagan administration's policies, people in poverty suffered cuts in government spending two and a half times greater than those of all other groups combined (Harrington, 1984).

Funding Reductions for Housing. The Housing Act of 1949 marked the beginning of federal assistance to provide decent housing for all citizens. The Act declared this as a national goal. Since the late 1970's, however, the federal government has removed itself from the housing issue (Dillingham, Geake, DiNello, Cropsey & Cherry, 1987; Dreier, 1987). Federal housing programs for the poor have been cut 76% since 1981 (Barancik, 1989; Dreier, 1987; National Coalition for the Homeless, 1988). While in office, the Reagan administration eliminated most housing programs existing in 1980. For example, the component of Section 8 which provided for construction of new low-cost housing was terminated in 1983, and the budget of the Department of Housing and Urban Development (HUD) was reduced from $30 billion in 1980 to $10 billion in 1987 (Dillingham et al., 1987).

This reduction in housing programs has been directed at low-income households, not to the public in general. In 1989, 52% of all housing subsidies went to households with incomes greater than $50,000, while only 16% of the housing subsidies went to households with incomes less than $10,000 (American Public Welfare Association, 1989). Nationwide, only 36% of the 7.5 million low-income renters in 1989 received a rental subsidy from a federal, state, or local housing program or lived in public housing (Leonard & Lazere, 1992).

This trend of the federal government withdrawing its responsibility for low-cost housing began in 1979. In that year, Congress began approving reductions in federal funding for housing and left the issue to the states. The Reagan administration coined the term "devolution" to describe the new trend of transferring responsibility from the federal government to states, cities, and counties (Dillingham et al., 1987; Marotto & Friedland, 1987).

Funding Reductions for Income Support. This trend has also occurred in U.S. welfare policies. Eligibility requirements for federal assistance programs became much more restrictive under the Reagan administration (Bassuk & Lauriat, 1984). Millions of people had their benefits reduced or eliminated during the 1980's (Children's Defense Fund, 1989). Between 1981 and 1986, 442,000 people were dropped from federal programs (Marcuse, 1988). Food Stamps were cut $6.8 billion from 1982 to 1988, with 1 million people losing eligibility and 20 million more receiving reductions (Marcuse, 1988). Only by late 1988 was legislation passed to restore the level of food stamp benefits (*Safety Network*, 1988a).

From 1970 to 1987, the average value of Aid to Families with Dependent Children (AFDC) benefits fell by 35% to only 44.2% of the poverty line. In 41 states in 1988, the combined value of AFDC and Food Stamps was less than 75% of the poverty level, and the AFDC housing allowance in all but seven states covered less than half of the federally defined "fair market rent" (National Coalition for the Homeless, 1988). In 1987, the percentage of unemployed citizens receiving unemployment insurance benefits reached a record low-- only 31.5% received any, leaving 5.1 million jobless people without benefits (*Safety Network*, 1988b). By the recession of 1991, this percentage had increased to only 42%, and the emergency unemployment compensation program enacted in November of that year has fallen far short of returning unemployment insurance protection to adequate levels (Shapiro & Nichols, 1992).

Federal government policies have also hurt the working poor. The real value of the minimum wage was $2.30 per hour in 1977; it had dropped to $1.88 per hour in 1988 (Marcuse, 1988). The low minimum wage, raised in April 1990 for the first time since 1981, has left many working families in poverty (Barancik, 1989). In 1992, full-time, year-round work at the minimum wage of $4.25 paid only 78% of the poverty line for a family of three, and only slightly more than 60% of the poverty line for a family of four (Hutchinson, Lav & Greenstein, 1992).

Funding Reductions by State Governments. In more recent years, a similar trend toward cutting social programs for people in poverty has been emerging in state governments. This has been occurring primarily in response to the serious fiscal crises that states are now facing, brought on in part by the federal government's "devolution" policies.

In order to reduce their deficits, states have been cutting spending, and much of this has been directed at programs serving impoverished people. For two consecutive years, state programs assisting low-income people have been sharply cut (Lav, Gold, Lazere & Greenstein, 1993). In 1992, 44 states froze or cut AFDC benefits; this followed similar reductions in 40 states in 1991. States have also made severe cuts in general cash assistance programs which have affected nearly half a million people nationwide. Eight states reduced or eliminated General Assistance (GA) benefits in 1992; fourteen states had made similar cutbacks in 1991 (Lav, et al., 1993). In some states, the cuts were very severe, involving the elimination of benefits for large numbers of people. In Michigan alone, 82,000 people are now eligible for no cash assistance from any level of government following the elimination of the state's GA program in 1991 (Shapiro, Gold, Sheft, Strawn, Summer & Greenstein, 1991).

The potential ramifications of such dramatic cuts are illustrated by a study by the Urban Institute which found that GA plays a crucial role in preventing homelessness. The study of 147 cities found that the cities experiencing the most homelessness were those without any GA program. The cities with limited GA programs had an intermediate degree of homelessness, and those with broad GA programs had much lower levels (Leonard & Lazere, 1992).

Two studies in Michigan provide further evidence of the link between GA cutbacks and homelessness. The Center for Urban Studies at Wayne State University has estimated that more than one-third of the former Michigan GA recipients had been evicted for non-payment of rent and had no regular place to live following their termination of benefits (Lav, et al., 1993). Another study, which surveyed nearly 55,000 of the former recipients, indicated that homelessness and hunger had increased among this population, with more than 20,000 of them having no regular place to stay and 27,000 of them going hungry. In addition, the study found that the labor market was not able to absorb the former recipients. Only 17% of them were working at six months after they had been dropped from the welfare rolls, with half of these in jobs that they had already had before losing GA (Michigan League for Human Services, 1992).

Conclusion

Funding cutbacks in government programs to serve the poor have been especially devastating because they have occurred in conjunction with other structural changes in the economy, housing market, and political system. Trends in these areas have converged to create a dramatic transformation of the U.S. social structure--one which is resulting in growing disparity between rich and poor and a lack of affordable housing for people living in poverty.

An awareness of the structural changes which have transformed our society reveals that homelessness can be viewed as one symptom of those changes. The fact that homelessness can be traced to structural sources attests to the political nature of the issue. Changes in the economy, housing market, and political system have directly benefitted those in elite classes, and this is precisely the reason the changes have occurred. The interests of those victimized by the changes have been overlooked in the process. Government has intentionally sided with the interests of elite groups at the expense of low- and moderate-income people.

Government's Response to Homelessness

Government has catered to the interests of elite groups not only by implementing conservative policies, but by propagating conservative ideology which has served to justify inequality and keep impoverished people docile and self-blaming. The response to homelessness is an example of these efforts. Throughout the 1980's and early 1990's, a common response by policy-makers has been to try to minimize the problem by attributing blame to homeless people themselves. Such a victim-blaming strategy serves to protect the interests of elite groups by diverting attention from the structural sources of social problems and encouraging the public to view victims of the problems as irresponsible or deficient in some way (Ryan, 1971).

The victim-blaming response to homelessness has in fact been very successful at deluding the public into believing that homeless people are to blame for their own condition. Social science research has played a major role in propagating this idea. Numerous research studies have examined "deviant" characteristics of homeless people, such as mental illness and substance abuse, and defined these characteristics as the cause of homelessness. These research findings provided policy-makers with a rationale for the growing homelessness problem and a justification for ignoring the structural conditions giving rise to the problem. The media also played a role in propagating victim-blaming ideas by promoting similar characterizations of homeless people. The result of this victim-blaming ideology has been a widespread lack of awareness about the structural sources of homelessness and a corresponding lack of awareness about the politics of the issue.

The point being made here is not that characteristics such as mental illness and substance abuse do not exist in the homeless population. Rather, the point is that focusing on these characteristics misrepresents the homelessness problem. There is no question that changes in U.S. social structure have increased the poverty rate, lowered the incomes of people in middle-income and impoverished classes, and dramatically reduced the supply of low-cost housing. Many kinds of people have been affected by these structural changes. One reason that people exhibiting "deviant" characteristics exist in the homeless population is because it is often the most vulnerable groups in our society which are first to fall victim to such changes. Another reason is that the reality of being homeless can create such "deviant" behavior in people. Living on the street is probably as much a cause of mental illness and substance abuse as it is an effect.[1] But perhaps the most significant point to be made is that these groups constitute only a portion of the homeless population. There are many other homeless people whose condition cannot be similarly "pathologized." These are the people that victim-blaming researchers and policy-makers disregard in their accounts. There is no way to explain their presence in the homeless population using a victim-blaming perspective.

The victim-blaming tradition served the interests of the Reagan and Bush administrations by providing a justification for the homelessness problem and by diverting attention from structural sources of growing inequality. Under this tradition, responding to homelessness became a matter of charity, as revealed by Former President Bush's call for "1000 points of light" to solve problems of poverty and inequality. People in poverty came to no longer be seen as an oppressed group with rights, as they were regarded by many in the 1960's and 1970's, but as inferior individuals who were at best pitied, and at worst despised.

The election of Clinton may mark the beginning of a transition to more progressive attitudes and policies, but the administration's intentions in the area of poverty are not completely clear at this point. It is likely that a dramatic process of consciousness-raising will be needed to break through the victim-blaming ideology which has prevailed for more than a decade. The occurrence of such a process, however, would probably require the emergence of a Homeless and Poor People's Movement. Widespread consciousness-raising does not occur in the abstract, but within the context of social movements. A movement of homeless and poor people could potentially break through victim-blaming ideologies and work to promote a political awareness of homelessness and poverty. The emergence of such a movement is the topic of the following chapter.

Note

[1]For a discussion of the problem of attributing homelessness to mental illness and other "pathologies," see the bibliography for Snow, Baker & Anderson (1988) and Snow, Baker, Anderson & Martin (1986).

Chapter 3

The Homeless
and Poor People's Movement

While most people have been relatively quiescent in response to the recent changes in social class structure, there are signs of growing discontent. The rebellion in Los Angeles and other cities in spring of 1992 is one very visible and dramatic demonstration of this discontent.

Other more organized protests have also occurred. Unions of the Homeless, Welfare Rights Unions, and Up and Poverty Now chapters, have arisen in the past decade. These are grassroots organizations comprised of or led by homeless and other low-income people. The first Union of the Homeless was formed in Philadelphia in 1983 by a homeless man named Chris Sprowal. According to Leona Smith, the president of the National Union of the Homeless, unions now exist in twenty-three cities across the country.

Welfare Rights groups first appeared in the mid-1960's, as impoverished people banded together to challenge the public relief system. The groups were joined together in the National Welfare Rights Organization (Piven & Cloward, 1977). In response to growing hardship in the 1980's, the organization was reconstituted, and the National Welfare Rights Union was formed in 1987. Today, Welfare Rights Unions exist in more than thirty cities (Kramer, 1993).

Up and Out of Poverty Now, which is a coalition of more than 300 groups, had its origins in Boston when a welfare rights group tried in 1985 to force the state of Massachusetts to abide by its legal requirement to maintain public assistance grants at the poverty level

(Bernard, 1992). Up and Out of Poverty Now was officially formed two years later at a Survival Summit in Philadelphia. According to Marian Kramer, the national president of the organization, the coalition works for economic and social justice both in the U.S. and internationally.

These grassroots protest organizations are involved in efforts to force policy-makers to represent the interests of people in poverty. Protest strategies have included both conventional and unconventional tactics. The groups have tried to work within the system to create change through lobbying efforts, but have also worked outside of the system in attempts to force policy-makers to respond. Two of the most common confrontational strategies the groups have used involve taking over abandoned government-owned housing and constructing tent cities.

The formation of these protest organizations constitute the beginnings of what could become a widespread Homeless and Poor People's Movement in this country. One might expect that as the number of homeless and poor people continues to increase, these groups will grow in number and strength. This chapter explores the possibility of the development of such a protest movement. In the first section, the case is made that conditions appear conducive for a widespread movement to occur. Subsequent sections discuss potential forms of protest that an emerging movement could take, potential successes of the movement, and possible limitations on the movement's success.

The Potential for an Emerging Movement

The emergence of a protest movement is a rare and complex phenomenon, and it is not the intent of this book to predict with any certainty that a widespread movement will occur. Rather, the analysis focuses on the potential for the occurrence of such a movement, given current structural conditions.

The emergence of protest movements requires dramatic individual and collective transformations. People who for years or entire lifetimes quietly endured oppression, come to question the legitimacy of the social structure and to rebel against their oppressors. The phenomenon signifies a tremendous transformation of consciousness and behavior. In order to try to explain these personal and political transformations, many social movement theorists point to the role of the social structure. Social movement theory suggests that massive changes in structural conditions can serve as an impetus for protest movements.

Structural Sources of Protest

Piven and Cloward (1977) have divided theories on the structural sources of protest movements into two categories: those that focus on pressures that encourage unrest and those that focus on the breakdown of society's regulatory capacity. "Pressure" theorists emphasize economic change as a precondition for unrest and protest. Periods of rapid and dramatic economic change often result in people receiving less than they expect--either during periods of economic improvement which generate rising expectations or when new and unexpected economic hardship occurs. These ideas have also been associated with a broader theory of relative deprivation which suggests that people may feel that they do not have what they need or deserve in comparison to a reference group (Benyon, 1987; Korpi, 1974; Lea & Young, 1984). Whether the focus is on rising expectations, increased hardship, or relative deprivation, this theoretical perspective points to the resulting increase in frustration and anger as an explanation for protest.

The second category of structural sources of protest focuses on the breakdown of the regulatory capacity of institutions as a precondition for protest. These theorists suggest that periods of massive economic change tend to weaken the ability of social institutions to regulate the lives of individuals by displacing people from the realm of mainstream institutional influence and destroying the structures of daily life. Once people are displaced from the realm of institutional influence, they are set free from prevailing systems of social control.

Some theorists have termed this displacement process "political marginalization" and have specifically linked it to a more fundamental process of economic marginalization (Lea & Young, 1984). In industrialized countries, employment serves as a fundamental regulating structure for most people during ordinary times. But when employment is not available for some people, the institution of work can no longer regulate their ideas and behavior. Since work and the ability to earn a living underpins the stability of other institutions as well, other realms of behavior can be affected (Piven & Cloward, 1977). For example, men who cannot support their families are more likely to abandon them, and people who cannot earn a living by legal means are more likely to pursue illegal means of survival. Communities experiencing long-term high unemployment can be devastated by their displacement from mainstream institutions. The first signs of change usually include rising crime, family breakdown, homelessness, and vandalism (Piven & Cloward, 1977).

As Piven and Cloward pointed out, economic change and the resulting displacement of people from institutional control, cannot entirely explain the emergence of protest. A transformation of consciousness must also occur. People must come to perceive the hardships they are experiencing as unjust and develop a corresponding sense of efficacy to confront and rectify the injustice (Piven & Cloward, 1977). In order for this transformation to occur, a process of "disindoctrination" (Vio Grossi, 1981) must take place. Oppressed people have been indoctrinated with the dominant ideology, which justifies their oppression and blames them for their problems instead of the system. This happens through a process Freire (1970) called the "doctrine of personal culpability," an ideological schema which encourages and predisposes people to interpret their failures as evidence of personal deficit. Disindoctrination involves unmasking these myths propagated by ideology.

Mass disindoctrination of oppressed groups and the transformation of consciousness it spurs are rare historical events, but there are several structural factors which can influence its occurrence (Piven & Cloward, 1977). The first is the number of people who are affected by the problem. The greater the number of people experiencing hardship, the more likely it is that people will view the problem as a collective one and attribute blame for it to the larger social structure rather than to themselves. The second factor is the stability of the broader social structure. When social institutions themselves begin to malfunction--for example, factories shut down, banks fail, or government becomes inept or corrupt--it becomes easier for people to question the legitimacy of social conditions.

A third factor concerns the behavior of elite classes during these periods of institutional upheaval. Economic and institutional change affects members of elite classes in different ways--some may gain power while others lose it. If the shift in power is dramatic enough, elites may divide among themselves. In their continued struggle for power, some in the elite classes may attempt to enlist the support of impoverished groups by giving validation to their grievances. If this occurs, it can serve to raise the hopes of impoverished people, while simultaneously creating visible dissention among elites which further undermines their authority and the legitimacy of social institutions (Piven & Cloward, 1977).

Present Structural Conditions

Economic Pressures

The information provided in the previous chapter vividly illustrates the dramatic changes which have been occurring in U.S. social structure in recent years. The relocation of manufacturing plants to other countries, as well as increasing automation, have resulted in a trend toward deindustrialization and a corresponding displacement of many workers from well-paying jobs. Changes in the housing market have eroded the low-cost housing supply, resulting in a situation of housing "haves" and "have-nots" (Apgar, DiPasquale, Cummings & McArdle, 1990). The "Reagan Revolution" of the 1980's brought a return of "trickle-down" economics and reduced government expenditure on social programs--a situation which has benefitted the wealthy and devastated the poor. These economic and political trends have resulted in a dramatic transformation of the social class structure--one in which the gap between rich and poor has substantially widened. The new American society is characterized by poverty amidst wealth and a visible and ever-increasing population of individuals who cannot afford housing.

These changes have meant that many people are receiving much less than what they had come to expect. With the decrease in the number of manufacturing jobs, many people who once earned middle-income wages have now been forced into low-paying service employment. Since the middle of this century (due primarily to the struggles of the Labor Movement), employment in manufacturing has offered workers the opportunity to earn a good living. This expectation has been passed down in many families from one generation to the next. With increasing numbers of plant shut-downs and layoffs, these workers have had their expectations violated. Many of these people may view these changes as temporary setbacks resulting from a depressed economy. But as increasing numbers of these displaced workers sink into poverty and come to recognize that they will not regain their previous jobs and standard of living, it can be expected that their anger and frustration will grow.

In addition to laid-off industrial workers, many lower-income people who have lived in poverty their entire lives have received less than what they had come to expect. Poverty has always been a devastating experience, but the Great Society programs of the 1960's had offered low-income groups some relief from their hardship and some additional opportunities. Throughout the 1980's, this relief was withdrawn as the Reagan/Bush administrations slashed social programs and implemented conservative economic and fiscal policies. The experience of poverty is a much more devastating condition for many people today than it was in the late 1960's and 1970's. As outlined in the previous chapter, the real income of people in poverty has dropped; and the withdrawal of government resources from low-income communities, as well as changes in the economy, have meant that there are few opportunities for escape.

One other significant change in the lives of low-income people involves the lack of affordable housing. Homelessness had not been a widespread problem in recent decades. Not since the Great Depression of the 1930's has the homeless population been as large as it is today (Hopper, Susser, Conover, 1985). Similar to that era, tent and shanty settlements (known as Hoovervilles in the 1930's, and often referred to as Bushvilles today) have emerged in major U.S. cities. Changes in the economy, housing market, and political system have re-created a society in which low-income people must contend either with the reality of homelessness or the constant, looming threat of it.

Only the passing of time will reveal whether the frustration and anger generated from violated expectations will be sufficient to spur a widespread protest movement. But if history is any indication, it is noteworthy that previous "capitalist heydays" (Phillips, 1992) like that of the 1980's, were marked by growing unrest and protest. There were numerous violent protests and strikes throughout the Gilded Age period (Boase, 1980; Goldberg, 1991; Phillips, 1992; Piven & Cloward, 1977), and the modern Labor Movement arose from the protest which occurred in the aftermath of the Roaring Twenties (Goldberg, 1991; Piven & Cloward, 1977; McCammon, 1990).

Potential Changes in Government Policy. The emergence of a movement may be partially contingent upon the actions of the new Clinton-Gore administration and Congress. While the new policy-makers can be expected to create change, it is unclear at this point how substantial that change will be. Unless the policy-makers can significantly curtail the trends which are transforming the social structure or at least counteract their adverse effects, they may have little success at alleviating hardship and thereby reducing the likelihood of protest.

Clinton has proposed a variety of initiatives designed to improve the economy and create progressive change. It is unclear at this point which of these initiatives will actually be enacted by Congress. In these early days of his administration, Clinton has encountered much opposition to his programs from Republicans and conservative Democrats. If this opposition continues, it is clear that very little change will be created and the likelihood of protest will potentially increase.

Even if Clinton has more success in the future getting his proposals passed, the changes created may be insufficient to discourage protest. The analysis below examines Clinton's original proposals and their potential for creating meaningful progressive change. While Clinton has already retreated on some of these original initiatives, they are included in the analysis because they represent a "best case" scenario. Any future initiatives are likely to be even less substantial.

A foundation of Clinton's economic plan is the creation of high-paying jobs in both the private and public sectors. Clinton's proposals for creating private sector jobs have included: providing investment tax credits for business, providing a special capital gains tax break for investments in small businesses held at least five years, developing enterprise zones in impoverished areas, changing bank-lending regulations to make loans more accessible to small businesses, and reducing tax breaks for corporations which move production plants to other countries.

While these policies could help create general economic improvement and create some additional jobs, they would probably do little to address the structural economic trend toward deindustrialization arising from increased automation and corporate flight. Curtailing this trend could in fact be an impossible task. Preventing corporate flight, for example, would be difficult because it would be hard to offer incentives that are more enticing to corporations than the prospect of cheap labor and minimal environmental and other regulatory restrictions offered in other countries.

Clinton's proposals appear in fact to reflect an understanding of these limitations. His original proposals clearly favored small businesses--by providing them with more significant tax incentives and by raising tax rates only on very large corporations (those with taxable incomes of more than $10 million). Small businesses have been the primary source of job creation in the U.S., due in part to corporate flight and downsizing by large companies, and Clinton apparently would like to focus his efforts on strengthening the trend toward small business job creation, instead of on attempting to curtail the trend toward deindustrialization.

While such a policy of favoring small businesses would likely be beneficial in the long-term, problems would almost certainly remain in the short-term. It is unlikely that the economic stimulus would be able to offset the adverse consequences of corporate flight and downsizing. As large corporations continue to lay off hundreds of thousands of workers, it would be difficult to generate enough new jobs in small businesses to replace those lost. This situation will be further aggravated by government cuts in such areas as the defense industry, which are leading to even more job loss.

The trend toward corporate flight and downsizing among large corporations, therefore, will inevitably create problems for the U.S. economy. Since it is unrealistic to try to stop this trend, perhaps the best strategy would be one of attempting to slow its pace. Clinton's proposal to reduce tax breaks for corporations which move production sites to other countries is an example of such a strategy.

But working against such efforts to discourage corporate flight is Clinton's support of the North American Free Trade Agreement (NAFTA). As described in the previous chapter, NAFTA would eliminate barriers to the movement of capital and goods within the three North American countries, allowing multinational corporations even more flexibility to exploit cheap labor and avoid regulatory restrictions. The agreement would accelerate the trend toward corporate flight, resulting in further displacement of U.S. workers from well-paying jobs.

An additional consideration regarding Clinton's economic proposals concerns the wage levels of the new jobs created. Contrary to Clinton's goal, the private sector jobs which could be created through his initiatives may be primarily low-paying positions. Clinton had been counting on generating more manufacturing jobs as a mechanism for ensuring high wage levels, but as outlined above, this is an unlikely outcome. Indeed, some economists have advised Clinton that this goal is doomed to fail, saying that the new economy demands fewer manufacturing jobs and more service workers (Nasar,

1992).

Given that service jobs tend to pay less than manufacturing jobs, it can be expected that many of the jobs created will be low-paying. The creation of low-paying jobs may be a particular problem regarding Clinton's proposal to develop enterprise zones in impoverished areas. If such a policy is enacted, it can be expected that most businesses which set up operations in these areas will take advantage of the dire poverty and high unemployment rates and offer employees only minimum wages. In order to address the issue of private sector wage levels, Clinton would need to propose outright pro-labor policies, such as raising the minimum wage--policies that would meet considerable resistance in Congress if they were proposed.

Clinton's proposals to create public sector jobs could potentially have more success at creating high-paying positions. Clinton has proposed an economic program which would create jobs to rebuild U.S. infrastructure and develop better communication and environmental systems. If enacted, this job-creation plan could be a successful strategy for creating high-paying jobs. Creation of high-paying public sector jobs has in fact been suggested as a useful strategy for addressing the problem of low wages arising from current structural economic changes (Kuttner, 1983). It is not clear at this point, however, who the major beneficiaries of such a policy would be. It has been suggested that Clinton's proposals have been directed primarily at working class people who have become unemployed, not to the long-term poor (Gans, 1992).

In addition to economic growth programs, Clinton has proposed other changes in government policies to address the trend toward growing inequality. For example, Clinton would like to change Federal Reserve Board policies to allow the rate of money expansion to grow. This change would reverse the conservative tight money supply policies which have facilitated the trend toward a less equitable distribution of wealth. This change, however, is ultimately out of Clinton's direct control. The final decision lies with Alan Greenspan, the Republican who chairs the board until 1996 and is responsible for previous conservative policies.

Early signs indicate a general willingness by Greenspan to support Clinton's initiatives, although the signs are somewhat mixed. Greenspan so far has maintained previous tight money policies--deciding to actually reduce the rate of growth in the money supply for 1993 (Greenhouse, 1993). The tightening effect of these policies may be offset by other policy decisions which support Clinton's initiatives, such as reducing interest rates--although the continuation of this policy is periodically threatened by reports of growing inflation.

Clinton's proposals to create a more progressive income tax system offer another example of efforts to reverse conservative fiscal policies and work toward a more equitable distribution of wealth. Clinton's original proposals included: increasing the top tax rate from 31% to 36% (affecting individuals with taxable incomes of more than $115,000 and couples with taxable incomes of more than $140,000); adding a 10% surtax on households with taxable incomes of more than $250,000; requiring wealthy households to pay Medicare tax on all earned income by lifting the current $135,000 ceiling; raising the top corporate tax rate from 34% to 36%; and limiting business deductions involving meals and entertainment, club dues, lobbying expenses, and executive pay above $1 million per year. While some of these original proposals have since been scaled back (such as the tax rate increase on corporations), the proposals nevertheless represent a substantial shift from previous conservative policies.

In addition to changes in fiscal and economic policies, Clinton's proposals have also included policy changes to address poverty and the low-cost housing shortage. Overall, Clinton's plan is favorable to low-income people, although it contains some serious weaknesses, especially regarding low-cost housing policies (Greenstein & Leonard, 1993).

While some housing policy initiatives in the plan would lead to improvements in the low-cost housing situation, these changes would be offset to a great extent by cuts in other housing programs. The progressive initiatives included in Clinton's original plan were: providing a one-time increase of $2.5 billion to the Community Development Block Grant program (some of which would likely be used for housing); providing a $423 million supplemental appropriation for the Supportive Housing Program for the Homeless (a grant program to provide housing and services to homeless people); increasing funding to renovate deteriorating public housing and privately-owned, federally-subsidized housing; providing for a modest increase in the number of low-income households receiving rental subsidies (by 40,000 households in fiscal year 1993 to 100,000 in fiscal year 1998); and permanently extending the low-income housing tax credit (Greenstein & Leonard, 1993).

Countering these progressive initiatives were other proposed changes to cut low-cost housing programs. Under Clinton's plan,

1994 appropriations for the Department of Housing and Urban Development's low-cost housing programs would be reduced to $745 million below fiscal year 1993 levels, adjusting for inflation. While appropriations would then increase over the next five years, funding allocations would be diverted from housing programs serving the poor to programs serving somewhat higher-income groups (Greenstein & Leonard, 1993). Several programs designed specifically to serve the poor, such as construction of public housing, would be terminated and replaced by a block grant housing program (HOME) which is likely to focus to a greater extent on higher-income households. The net result of these funding changes would be an overall reduction of funds of $5.9 billion over the next five years (Greenstein & Leonard, 1993).

In addition to these changes, further reductions to housing programs would occur through a proposal to place a new limit on the amount of subsidy provided to private owners of subsidized housing projects whose contracts are about to expire. Such a change in policy could encourage some owners to convert their buildings into other, more profitable uses, instead of entering into new contracts--a situation that would lead to the displacement of current low-income residents (Greenstein & Leonard, 1993).

Since cuts in housing programs and changes in funding allocations would largely offset the plan's progressive initiatives, Clinton's plan would likely make little or no progress in remedying the low-cost housing crisis. The National Law Center on Homelessness and Poverty (1993) has suggested in fact that Clinton's plan could lead to an overall reduction in affordable housing for low-income people. This continued government neglect of the low-cost housing problem will undoubtedly result in a continuing increase in the number of homeless people. While Clinton's proposals to address poverty in general (described below) could potentially result in some minor alleviation of homelessness, the problem could not be meaningfully addressed without substantial progressive measures to restore the low-cost housing supply.

Clinton's proposals to address poverty in general have been somewhat more progressive than his housing policy proposals. His original anti-poverty proposals included (in addition to enterprise zones and general economic improvement): expanding the Earned Income Tax Credit for full-time and part-time workers; providing full funding for Head Start and WIC (a supplemental food program for women, infants, and children) and improving childhood immunization programs; expanding Food Stamp benefits and low-income energy assistance; providing a modest increase in funds for child care assistance to low- and moderate-income families; creating community development banks to provide loans for business and housing development in impoverished areas; improving the public education system; providing loans for all students who want to go to college; expanding the Job Corps; and implementing an apprenticeship program for non-college bound students.[1]

While these proposals are a considerable improvement over previous conservative policies, they are still limited in scope and therefore would not create very substantial change, especially in the short-term. For example, while the Earned Income Tax Credit can be a good policy for addressing poverty among working people, the policy would need to be expanded beyond Clinton's proposals in order for it to have a significant effect on the lives of impoverished people. For full-time workers with children, Clinton originally proposed expanding the credit to make up the difference between the families' earnings and the poverty line. Such a policy change would have little impact, considering the federal government's definition of poverty. For example, in 1993 the federal government's criteria for living in poverty was $6,810 or less for an individual, $9,190 or less for a household of two, $11,570 or less for a household of three, and $13,950 or less for a household of four.   While raising incomes to the poverty line would be of some help to impoverished people, it would do little to substantially improve their living conditions. Much of the gains in fact would merely offset Clinton's proposed energy taxes. In order for Clinton's proposals to have a significant impact, the federal government's criteria for poverty would need to be raised to more realistic levels.[2]

Clinton's proposals also fail to adequately address the income needs of those who would remain unemployed despite job-creating policies. Clinton's welfare to work proposal may account for some of these unemployed people, but the success of this program in both fiscal and social terms is partially contingent upon the availability of private sector jobs.   Clinton's plan includes providing welfare recipients with education, training, and child care for up to two years, and then forcing them into either private sector or community service jobs. Gans (1992) has pointed out that creating jobs for welfare recipients is actually more costly than providing direct benefits, and this will certainly prove to be true if a large number of public sector jobs must be provided to former recipients due to scarcity of private sector jobs. And if the Earned Income Tax Credit is not expanded to a greater degree, the welfare to work program will not offer these former recipients substantially higher standards of living, but will merely add them to the ranks of the working poor.

There is an additional danger in this proposal that the program will be approved by Congress, but that sufficient funding will not be allocated to carry out the education and training components, as well as the provision of community service jobs. If this happens, the program will ultimately serve to just drop many recipients from the welfare rolls and into even more extreme poverty. Such an outcome would cause the homeless population to burgeon and would undoubtedly lead to growing unrest.

Gans (1992) has suggested that adequately addressing the income needs of the unemployed requires the implementation of a universal income grant program to go to all people who are part of the labor surplus. He explains that there is a European principle of not allowing the incomes of the poor to fall below 60% or 70% of the median income, and suggests that the fact that U.S. welfare recipients receive on average only one-fifth of the nation's median income partially accounts for the marginalization of the poor and resulting social problems, such as high crime rates.

Overall, Clinton's original initiatives would offer some alleviation of hardship for people in poverty. In practical terms, however, the changes created would be unlikely to have a substantial impact on homelessness and poverty. During this time of deindustrialization and corporate downsizing, it would probably be impossible to combat this trend toward growing inequality without a significant outlay of government resources, as well as a dramatic shift in government policy to favor the interests of labor and impoverished groups over those of more privileged groups.

Given the inclination of policy-makers to serve the interests of their powerful constituencies, it is unlikely that Clinton would propose--or that Congress would approve--such progressive policies. Clinton won the election by appealing to the middle classes or those previously in the middle classes, and his proposals for economic improvement are targeted primarily at these groups. People in poverty will be the easiest group for Clinton and other policy-makers to overlook, since they do not comprise a powerful constituency. In addition, it still remains politically fashionable to blame the poor for their condition and to dismiss many as "undeserving" (Gans, 1992).

The subgroup of the poor which appears to be viewed as deserving by the new administration is impoverished children. A large portion of the administration's anti-poverty proposals are directed specifically at children. While Clinton has proposed some programs to address the interests of long-term poor adults, his attitudes toward these individuals appear to be somewhat blaming and punitive, as reflected by his welfare reform proposals and by his lecturing to African American audiences about becoming more "responsible" (Knoll, Rocawich, Conniff & Buell, 1992).

Clinton's political background helps explain why his anti-poverty proposals have been somewhat moderate and why they will likely continue to be. While Clinton appointed some liberals to his cabinet, he has described himself as part of the new Democratic Party, which opposes much of the liberal philosophy. Clinton in fact recently led the organization which was founded to criticize and change the liberal tradition in the Democratic Party: the Democratic Leadership Council. And while there have been behind-the-scenes confrontations between the opposing factions regarding such policies as welfare reform (DeParle, 1992), it is likely, given Clinton's background in the new tradition, that his policies will ultimately reflect this new school of thought.

Clinton's reaction to congressional opposition to his proposals seems to support this outcome. Clinton is clearly assuming more moderate positions in order to get his proposals passed. He has already scaled back some of the progressive elements of his economic and budget packages, and at the time of this writing was also considering including regressive measures, such as limiting spending on federal entitlement programs.

In terms of coming to power and remaining in power, the new Democratic tradition in a sense can be seen as more practical in today's society than the liberal tradition. It is unlikely that a liberal Democrat would have been able to win the presidency. This recognition points to the limitations of even well-intentioned policy-makers in creating progressive change. While such limitations have existed throughout U.S. history, the obstacles are perhaps even more severe today than in recent decades due to shifting power relations among social classes. Events which have spurred the structural changes in our country have simultaneously resulted in a tremendous increase in the power of the corporate world. Advances in technology which have reduced the need for human labor and have allowed corporations to transfer production sites from one country or region to another, have shifted the balance of power markedly to the side of big business. The power of industrial labor in every country has been severely undermined, and so too has government's ability to exert meaningful control over corporate activities.

The problems confronting the U.S. and the world today are not issues of lack of wealth, but rather its inequitable distribution. Powerful corporations worldwide have profited by exploiting cheap labor, avoiding regulatory restrictions, and automating production. Workers in both "developed" and Third World countries have suffered as a result. Governments are now limited in enforcing the rights of industrial workers--even if they wanted to--because of the ability of corporations to transfer production sites elsewhere. Similarly, governments are constrained in taxing corporations, and often must provide them with tax incentives for investing in a particular country or region. Ratification of NAFTA and the global free trade proposals under the General Agreement on Tariffs and Trade (GATT) will shift the balance of power even further to the side of corporations. Clinton appears at times to understand his predicament in trying to ensure the well-being of ordinary citizens while simultaneously catering to business interests. For example, during a campaign argument over the NAFTA, Clinton expressed concern about the U.S. workers who would lose their jobs if the agreement were enacted, but in the end supported the agreement in principle (Walsh, Cooper & Robbins, 1992).

The only way for governments of the world to reclaim a meaningful degree of power over multinational corporations would be to work together to establish global regulations on business operations. Universal regulations regarding labor (such as minimum wage levels, working conditions and hours, and prohibitions on child labor), environmental contamination, and consumer health and safety standards, would allow governments to exercise a degree of control over multinationals. Such a move toward regulating multinational corporations would represent the exact opposite of the current free trade proposals in NAFTA and GATT, which are working toward global deregulation. The principal justification for the current proposals is the establishment of a "level playing field" for the world's corporations. Global policies which created universal regulations on multinationals, however, would accomplish this same goal, while simultaneously protecting against the exploitation of workers, consumers, and the environment. The obvious reason that the free trade proposals are working toward deregulation instead is that such a move favors the interests of corporations, and policy-makers tend to cater to the interests of these powerful groups. The natural allegiance of policy-makers is to their powerful constituencies, and these ties are broken only when protest by oppressed groups threatens societal stability (Piven & Cloward, 1977).

Given this reality of the U.S. political system, it is unlikely that Clinton and other policy-makers will enact policies which pose a serious challenge to the interests of corporations and other powerful groups. And if they do not, their attempts to make progressive change will be severely constrained. Significant alleviation of hardship would probably be impossible without a dramatic restructuring of power among social classes--a scenario which would demand that interests of elite groups be undermined.

It appears, therefore, that the new policy-makers may do little to lessen the likelihood of protest. In fact, the election of Clinton could serve to increase unrest because of the rising expectations that it generated. Many people in the country, including people in poverty, are relying on Clinton to transform the country and provide them with an opportunity for a better life. If conservative policy-makers continue to block the passage of Clinton's progressive initiatives, or if the policies which are enacted fail to create much change, it can be expected that the anger and frustration of impoverished groups will rise to even higher levels, thereby increasing the likelihood of protest.

Breakdown in Regulatory Capacity

As reviewed earlier, some social movement theorists point to the role of the breakdown in the regulatory capacity of social institutions as a precondition for the emergence of protest movements. It would be difficult to dispute that the first signs of this breakdown--rising crime, family breakdown, homelessness, and vandalism (Piven & Cloward, 1977)--exist today in the inner cities. Inner cities in the U.S. have deteriorated into subcultures of desperation and violence. Violent crime, drugs, gang warfare, and homelessness have all reached epidemic proportions and have created horrifying and desperate conditions for those who have no other choice but to live there.

With the changes in social structure in recent years, many people in the inner cities have been uprooted from the routines of ordinary life and displaced from the realm of mainstream institutions. Lack of employment opportunities has meant that large segments of the population are not under the influence of the regulatory capacity of work. For example, from 1978 to 1983, 70,000 manufacturing jobs disappeared from Watts and South Central Los Angeles. It has been estimated that at the time of the L.A. rebellion in spring of 1992, the African American male unemployment rate was about 40%. In fact, at no time since 1979 has the adult African American male national unemployment rate been under 10%. During this period it has been as high as 18.1%, and has averaged 12.9% (Wilkins, 1992).

High levels of unemployment have in turn undermined the regulatory capabilities of other institutions, such as family and schools. Indeed, a system of alternative "institutions" appears to have evolved. Cultures of gang violence and drugs, which promote different values than mainstream institutions, have arisen from the despair and hopelessness of inner-city realities. In a society which deprives inner-city, impoverished youth of any opportunities for a decent standard of living or a degree of freedom and security, drugs often become either an escape from the desperation or a means for earning a living, and a gun becomes a manifestation of power.

So far this breakdown in the regulatory capacity of mainstream social institutions has resulted primarily in isolated acts of disruption. As long as disruption is carried out by isolated individuals or small groups and occurs within the confines of low-income communities, it poses little threat to the greater society and can be ignored by policy-makers and other powerful groups. Once the disruption becomes collective, however, and either spills out into wealthier areas or has the potential for spilling out, a threat is created and policy-makers are forced to act. Such was the case during the rebellion in L.A. in spring of 1992.

The response to the rebellion by outsiders was revealing. Many people, especially those from white middle- and upper-income classes, were shocked by the insurgency. This is a reflection of how removed and protected these people are from the realities of the inner-city. The lack of comprehension of the rebellion and its causes was most vividly illustrated by the conservative response, which blamed the rioting on lack of family values. This simplistic analysis disregarded the role of economic and political transformations in creating the devastation of the inner-cities, and instead called for tighter social controls (stronger family values) as a means for quelling the unrest. This conservative response can be criticized not only on the grounds of being victim-blaming and unjust, but also for being an impossible solution. Since changes in social structure have removed many people in the inner-cities from the realm of mainstream institutional life, these people are no longer under the direct influence of these institutions. Propagating conservative ideology, therefore, can no longer serve as an effective mechanism for justifying inequality and keeping people docile.

It is a positive sign--and perhaps an indication of a changing public consciousness--that many other responses to the rebellion reflected an understanding of its root causes. Many insightful explanations of the rioting were articulated through the media, and calls for action to address the underlying issues were made. The fact that the truth was spoken and allowed to be spoken reflects a change from the 1980's, when such analyses were few and often denied credibility. There appears to be a growing awareness of the conditions of the inner-cities and the injustice of those conditions. In fact, the inner-city issue was cast into the presidential campaign--probably as a result of the L.A. rebellion--and the candidates were forced to acknowledge the problems and propose potential solutions. While the discourse by the candidates lacked meaningful analysis of the problems and their structural sources, the fact that the issue had pervaded mainstream politics was a sign of at least minimal progress.

Transformation of Consciousness

As outlined earlier, dramatic economic change and the resulting displacement of people from institutional control are not sufficient factors in themselves to spur a protest movement. There must be a corresponding transformation of consciousness which leads people to view their hardship as unjust and to develop a sense of efficacy to confront and rectify the injustice. As stated earlier, three factors which influence this transformation include: the number of people affected by the problems, the stability of the broader social context, and the behavior of elite classes (Piven & Cloward, 1977).

With the dramatic changes in social structure, increasing numbers of people are being displaced from well-paying jobs, are being forced into poverty, and are becoming homeless. Since the effects of these trends have only become apparent in recent years, many people may view their hardship as a temporary occurrence and may still have hope for regaining their previous standard of living. This may partially explain the quiescence of impoverished people up to this point. As the trends continue to transform the social structure, however, and ever-increasing numbers of people are adversely affected, the long-term nature of their hardship will become increasingly clear. Over time, as the number of people experiencing extreme hardship continues to grow, it will become more likely that people will attribute blame to the system and see it as unjust, thereby increasing the likelihood that a transformation of consciousness will occur.

A related factor in today's society which may facilitate this transformation is the dramatic and visible contrast between rich and poor. The wealth and extravagance of the rich is visible to the public, including people in poverty. Similarly, while many impoverished areas are somewhat hidden from public view, other signs of dire poverty are blatantly apparent. The epidemic of homelessness in major cities has resulted in this visible display of human hardship and suffering. As the number of homeless and impoverished individuals continues to grow, the stark contrast between rich and poor may become increasingly intolerable to the public in general, and to impoverished people in particular. The fact that millionaires and billionaires can flourish in a society that can offer no opportunities to masses of other individuals will provide a vivid illustration of inequality and injustice, making it easier for people to question the legitimacy of the social structure.

Instability in the broader social context is the second factor which influences a transformation of consciousness. The dramatic changes in social structure occurring today are not only resulting in personal hardship for isolated individuals--they are creating a society in which many mainstream institutions have begun to malfunction. In previous decades, the public had a relatively high degree of confidence in the social structure. Institutional arrangements appeared solid and stable, and many people were able to earn decent standards of living.

Today, in contrast, institutional operations are dramatically changing, leaving many people with a grave uncertainty about their future. Companies are shutting down production plants across the country and laying off hundreds of thousands of workers; corporate debt has skyrocketed and record numbers of corporations are filing for bankruptcy; Savings and Loans failed due to government ineptness and scandal by the rich; people are living on the street and in shelters because the housing market does not provide sufficient amounts of low-cost housing; a large portion of the public can no longer afford health care; the public educational system is failing to provide adequate education for many children and youth; and the federal government has amassed a huge debt which is stifling the economy and creating a tremendous tax burden for the country's citizens.

There appears to be a strong and growing awareness of this institutional malfunctioning among the public today. This awareness was reflected in, and perhaps sharpened by, the presidential campaign. The campaign was marked by a renewed interest in electoral politics. While many voters expressed displeasure with all of the presidential candidates, citizens were nevertheless much more involved in the political process than in recent years. Candidates were forced to address pertinent issues in the lives of ordinary people. Clinton capitalized on people's discontent and ended up winning with his theme of change, while Bush's strategy of pretending everything is really okay failed.

The messages of Clinton and Perot helped to heighten the public's awareness of institutional malfunctioning. Both Clinton and Perot focused to a great extent on the lack of well-paying jobs. Their focus on this issue made it very clear that changes in institutional functioning were responsible for the lack of jobs, thereby elucidating the fact that the system is to blame. Perot specifically cited the transferring of production sites to Mexico and other countries as a significant factor in the loss of U.S. manufacturing jobs. Perot's articulation of this point brought this economic reality out into public view.

Perot's criticism of government ineptness helped to highlight institutional malfunctioning even further. Perot unceasingly chastised the federal government for poor fiscal policies which have led to the huge federal debt and for nonexistent domestic policies to address society's numerous social problems. The public's skepticism and distrust of politicians were validated and heightened as a result of Perot's criticism, perhaps making people more open to questioning the legitimacy of social arrangements.

The above discussion relates to the third factor in a transformation of consciousness: the behavior of elite classes. In a struggle for power, some elites may try to win the support of impoverished groups by validating their grievances. This happened to some degree in the presidential campaign and continues to happen as Clinton attempts to push his policy initiatives through Congress. The social structure has been blamed for depriving people of well-paying jobs, for denying them health care, for catering to the interests of the rich at the expense of all others, and for burdening taxpayers with an exorbitant federal debt.

Most of this validation of grievances, however, has been focused on the hardships of people in middle-income classes (or those previously in the middle classes). With the exception of the plight of the inner-cities, little attention has been paid to the hardships of those living in extreme poverty, such as homeless people, or to those who have endured long-term poverty. Clinton in fact went out of his way during the campaign to demonstrate that he would not be co-opted by such "extremists" as Jessie Jackson or Sister Souljah who speak for the economically and racially oppressed.

Meaningful validation of the grievances of the most severely economically oppressed, as well as those of African Americans, Latino Americans, and Native Americans (who disproportionately comprise the impoverished classes), has yet to occur. The grievances of these groups have been validated only to the extent to which they overlap with the grievances of the middle classes. Nevertheless, many people in oppressed groups are now looking to the new administration to create changes that will improve their lives. If Clinton cannot produce changes to benefit people in poverty, the dynamics of class relations will change, and the resulting frustration and anger may lead to the emergence of protest.

As the situation evolves, there may be more pressure on policy-makers to respond to the grievances of people in poverty, and perhaps for them to side either with them or against them. This is the kind of situation former presidents Franklin Roosevelt and John Kennedy faced, as unrest grew during their respective eras. If Clinton would respond in the tradition of these Democratic presidents, he too would choose in the end to side with the oppressed and at that point would provide greater validation of their grievances.

Changes in Electoral Patterns

The fact that changes in electoral patterns took place in the last election may indicate in itself that the potential for a protest movement is growing. A sharp shift in traditional voting patterns has been identified as a first sign of popular discontent (Piven & Cloward, 1977). The electoral system serves to structure forms of protest in its early stages. People choose to show their discontent at the polls rather than in the streets. When policy-makers cannot fulfill people's expectations, however, protest may break out of the confines of the electoral system and meaningful defiance may occur (Piven & Cloward, 1977).

Dramatic shifts in traditional voting patterns were witnessed in the previous election. One meaningful change was simply the number of people who actually voted. Fifty-four percent of the total number of people in the eligible voting age range cast votes--the highest percentage since the Nixon/McGovern election twenty years earlier. Election results indicate other major changes, as well. In the presidential election, the 12-year reign of repressive Republican administrations was finally overturned. In the Senate, the number of women elected reached an all-time high of six (up from two), and the first African American woman was elected, as well as the first Native American in sixty years. In the House of Representatives, dramatic changes also occurred. The biggest turnover since 1948 took place, with 24 incumbents losing their seats. With the number of representatives who lost in the primaries and those who retired figured in, this turnover translates into a total of 110 new representatives. With this turnover comes a major shift in the gender and racial composition of the House. The number of women increased from 28 to 47; the number of African Americans increased from 25 to 38; and the number of Latino Americans increased from 10 to 17. In addition to these changes, term limit propositions passed in each of the 14 states in which they were proposed--yet another indication of growing discontent among the public.

Conclusion

It appears that some of the preconditions for the emergence of a protest movement exist today. Economic changes have dramatically altered the social class structure, resulting in people receiving less than they had come to expect and in the breakdown of the regulatory capacity of social institutions. It is not clear at this point if the changes will be sufficient to create enough anger and frustration, as well as a corresponding transformation of consciousness, necessary to spur a widespread movement. Signs of growing discontent--such as the L.A. rebellion, the formation of national grassroots protest organizations, and a shift in electoral patterns--are evident, but the ultimate outcome is uncertain. As discussed previously, the emergence of a widespread protest movement is partially contingent upon the actions of the new presidential administration and Congress. If the new elected officials in the federal government implement policies which result in a significant alleviation of hardship for many people, unrest may subside and a movement may be averted.

But if enough meaningful change is not made and present trends continue unabated, the potential for a protest movement will increase.

We are only beginning to experience the adverse effects of the massive changes occurring in our social structure. If steps are not taken to reverse the trends or lessen their devastating impact, masses of people will be affected. As time goes on, the middle class will further erode, and ever-increasing numbers of people will fall into poverty and become homeless, bringing U.S. society closer to the class structure of Third World countries (Barak, 1991).

Estimates of the homeless population today range from 230,000 to at least 3 million. By the end of the century, it is estimated that the homeless population will reach 19 million unless immediate action is taken to preserve and expand the low-cost housing supply (Barak, 1991). Most people would consider the homelessness problem today to be very severe; imagine what it would be like if there were more than six times as many homeless people forced into the streets.

If the homelessness and poverty problem were allowed to reach such monumental proportions, those affected would almost certainly react differently to their situation than most do today. Societal control over these individuals would increasingly decline, as they are further removed from the realm of mainstream institutional life. In an effort to survive, alternative communities and cultures would perhaps emerge. Instead of acting as isolated individuals as many do today, people would instead band together as more among them abandon all hope of re-entering mainstream society. Tent cities and shanty settlements, which are already developing in major cities, would become commonplace, and resources required for survival would probably be acquired by the means necessary.

Within such a scenario, it is difficult to imagine that a protest movement would not occur. The sheer numbers and the collective nature of the hardship, as well as the contrast between rich and poor, would facilitate the transformation of consciousness that is necessary for the emergence of protest. The fact that homelessness and poverty had been allowed to reach such catastrophic levels would reflect, if not create, further breakdown in institutional functioning within the broader society; and the turmoil which would inevitably exist in such a scenario would undoubtedly create further divisions among elites and force policy-makers to side either with those in poverty or against them.

Potential Forms of the Movement

If a widespread Homeless and Poor People's Movement does emerge, the forms of protest the movement would spawn are uncertain. It is unclear, for example, whether protest would be characterized by a cohesive, coordinated movement or by more spontaneous acts of disruption. One consideration is that the broad classification of Homeless and Poor People's Movement may actually include various factions of protesters, representing the many different segments of the population living in poverty.

The impoverished population can by no means be seen as a homogeneous group. The population is divided along various dimensions, including race, length of time in poverty, employment and educational status, and housing status. It is likely that protest would organize along these various dimensions. The emerging forms of protest would reflect to some degree the opportunities and resources available to these different groups.

Those with fewer resources and opportunities may simply riot and loot, as they did in L.A. While some social movement theorists distinguish between riots and movements, it can be argued that this distinction minimizes the significance of rioting as a form of protest and may reflect a bias of more privileged groups. As Reverend Martin Luther King, Jr. said, "A riot is the language of the unheard." Many of the poor are so isolated from mainstream societal institutions that the only opportunity they have for influence is civil disruption (Lea & Young, 1984; Piven & Cloward, 1977). Especially if riots occur within a context of mass upheaval and other organized forms of protest, a case can be made that they represent one aspect of the movement.

Development of a coordinated movement (as opposed to rioting) would require some level of resources and opportunities for organizing. Resource Mobilization theory, for example, suggests that movements can occur only when groups possess certain critical resources and opportunities for collective action (Gamson, 1990; Jenkins, 1983; McCarthy & Zald, 1977; Oberschall, 1973). While Resource Mobilization theory has been criticized for not applying to movements of impoverished people (Kerbo, 1982; Piven & Cloward, 1992), one resource that significantly influences the *form* of protest is group cohesion and solidarity. Some level of group cohesion is needed in order for a communications network to exist--a factor suggested as a necessary precondition for the development of coordinated movements (Freeman, 1983). Part of the success of the Southern Civil Rights Movement of the 1950's and 1960's can be attributed to the preexistence of solid community networks. Freeman (1983) has suggested that if a network does not exist or exists only in rudimentary form, one must be created in order for organizing efforts to proceed.

Given that there are currently minimal levels of political cohesiveness within the impoverished population, and even within the various factions of the population, significant change would need to occur in order for a coordinated protest movement to develop. If group solidarity is not enhanced before unrest reaches the point of widespread protest, the movement would probably be characterized mostly by spontaneous actions, at least in its early stages.

Potential for Developing Coordinated Protest

The potential for developing coordinated protest varies among the different factions of the population. The potential for some factions, especially those comprised of inner-city youth, currently appears dismal. Guns, gang warfare, and drugs have served to fragment the poor to a great extent in urban areas. Anger and frustration in these communities has been directed inward, causing young people to turn on each other instead of on those who oppress them.

Overcoming these internal divisions would require monumental change. A true consciousness-raising process within urban areas would need to occur. Given that the population in poverty is disproportionately comprised of racially oppressed groups, the greatest hope for overcoming these divisions and creating unity may be organizing efforts along racial lines. A resurgent African American Movement, for example, could work toward greater solidarity among African American people. African American unity has suffered great losses since the 1960's and early 1970's, but there appears to be a growing awareness of the collective nature of African American oppression and perhaps some signs of a shift toward greater solidarity. The recalling of the images and ideas of Malcolm X is one such sign. Perhaps even more significant is the current effort by some street gangs to end their rivalries and curb violence. In Los Angeles and Chicago, some of the country's most prominent gangs have called truces and have come together through campaigns, such as "Black Men United" and "United in Peace" (Muwakkil, 1993). While successfully overcoming existing divisions is likely to be a long-term struggle, these developments may reflect the beginnings of growing awareness and solidarity.

Other factions of the impoverished population may have more opportunities for building solidarity. Working people, for example, are drawn together in the workplace, facilitating the development of communication networks and encouraging the formation of a collective identity (Piven & Cloward, 1977). Working people may also have more incentive for building a coordinated protest because they have more potential for organized influence. Protest that affects institutions of importance to powerful groups is most likely to evoke responses from authorities (Piven & Cloward, 1977), and the central role of workers within businesses allows them the opportunity to have a significantly disruptive impact on business operations.

The working poor of today are primarily employed in service jobs, many of which pay considerably less than manufacturing jobs. The primary reason that service jobs tend to be low-paying is that many have not been unionized (Kuttner, 1983). Widespread unionization of manufacturing workers helped ensure high wages, and it is possible that a renewed labor movement could bring similar wage and benefit increases for service workers.

It is unclear how much of a struggle such a movement would require. Wage and benefit increases in manufacturing jobs required decades of protest by industrial workers, but the existence today of established labor unions--some of which represent service workers-- could facilitate the process. Working against such change, however, is the fact that the power of labor has been undermined due to both structural economic changes and conservative political policies. Now that big business has grown accustomed to its increased power over labor, it will undoubtedly be difficult for workers to force concessions from management. Depending on the responsiveness of new policy-makers to the lobbying of established unions, enhancement of worker's rights could require a powerful grassroots protest movement, similar perhaps to the industrial labor movement of the 1930's and 1940's. If a grassroots mobilization is necessary, it is possible that the beginnings of such a movement will emerge in the coming years, as structural economic changes continue to transform U.S. society.

While many among the homeless population are employed, homeless people as a group do not have similar resources and opportunities for creating a coordinated movement.   Building solidarity and exerting influence is often difficult for homeless protesters. The homeless population today can by no means be characterized as a cohesive group. The lives of many homeless people in fact have been marked by severe isolation. The emergence of Unions of the Homeless and the development of tent cities, however, may signify a transition toward growing group consciousness and cohesiveness. As the number of homeless people continues to grow and the prospect of re-entering mainstream society becomes increasingly dim, a class consciousness and group solidarity may naturally emerge as people band together for survival. The work of Unions of the Homeless, Welfare Rights Unions, Up and Out of Poverty Now, and other local grassroots organizations, may be instrumental in facilitating the development of group solidarity. As conditions become increasingly conducive for protest to occur, these organizations may help in creating a spirit of unity among homeless people. If some degree of solidarity can be established, the potential for developing a coordinated movement of homeless people will be enhanced.

In summary, the potential for building coordinated protest among the various factions of the impoverished population is contingent to a great extent on group solidarity and cohesiveness within the factions. If some level of solidarity can be achieved, the movement would perhaps be characterized by coordinated protest by various groups, such as homeless people, African Americans and other racially oppressed groups, and the working poor. If a meaningful level of solidarity cannot be achieved, however, the movement would more likely be characterized by spontaneous actions, such as those seen during the L.A. rebellion.

Potential Successes of the Movement

Even if a meaningful level of solidarity could be established, thereby making coordinated protest possible, protesters would need to determine where to focus their efforts in order to achieve the most significant changes. There is often an assumption that during periods of popular unrest, the most meaningful focus lies in developing formal, structured organizations which seek influence through conventional political channels. Followers of the Alinsky school of thought, for example, adhere to this belief (LeVeen, 1983). Others disagree with this assumption, arguing that the nature of poverty makes it impossible to use these conventional avenues.

Piven and Cloward (1977) advanced this alternative theory which suggests that people in poverty lack the financial and other resources and opportunities necessary to develop and maintain politically-influential organizations. Uprisings among the poor are always short-lived, and formal organizations usually disappear once the protest subsides, unless they have been co-opted by powerful groups. As the authors later pointed out, "To suppose that normal or conventional political strategies can have (dramatic effects for impoverished groups) is to underestimate the maldistribution of political resources and to trivialize the consequent realities of power" (Piven & Cloward, 1992, p. 319).

Based on their historical analysis of several social movements, Piven and Cloward (1977) suggest that a focus on building structured organizations minimizes the possibilities for creating change by channeling protest from disruption into bureaucratic activities. Given their marginalization in society, the most significant resource of people in poverty is their capacity to disrupt mainstream institutional functioning, and thereby force policy-makers to respond to their grievances. Piven and Cloward point to the successes of the Southern Civil Rights Movement of the 1950's and 1960's and the Industrial Workers Movement of the 1930's and 1940's, as examples of the effectiveness of mass disruption strategies.

This theoretical perspective suggests that a contemporary poor people's movement would be most successful in creating change if protesters engaged in disruptive actions rather than attempt to form permanent, formal organizations. But as Piven and Cloward point out, disruption is an effective strategy only during extraordinary historical moments when social unrest gives rise to new expectations and allows new forms of behavior. It will produce success only if policy-makers are both forced into responding to the disruption and are reluctant to use physical repression against the protesters. Reluctance to use repressive force will occur only if the grievances of the protesters can be shown to be legitimate, thereby generating public support for the protest movement (Piven & Cloward, 1977).

Public support of a movement, therefore, is a key to its success. Some social movement theorists have described how a movement's success at creating change is contingent upon the reaction of the middle third of the social class structure. When the middle third allies itself with the bottom third, instead of the top third, potential for progressive change is created. The reforms of the New Deal were possible, for example, because the newly-created liberal middle class came to support the interests of the working and impoverished classes (Epstein, 1990).

The public support factor may offer some insight into potential successes of various forms of protest which could arise from a widespread Homeless and Poor People's Movement. It is likely that the public would generally be more supportive of coordinated forms of disruption, rather than spontaneous actions such as those which occurred during the L.A. rebellion. While rioting and looting can help create more awareness of people's grievances, it is unlikely that the actions would generate much public support in the long-term, especially if they presented any threat to the well-being of more privileged groups.

It should be noted that while violence is commonly thought to be a characteristic of poor people's protest movements, generally speaking this is an incorrect assumption. Usually the risks involved in violence are too great for impoverished people to take (Piven & Cloward, 1977). When violence does occur in the context of protest, it is usually initiated by authorities in an effort to repress the actions of protesters (Goldberg, 1991; Piven & Cloward, 1977; Tilly, Tilly & Tilly, 1975). On those occasions when protesters do engage in violence, it is a reflection of how severely marginalized they are in society. It reflects their lack of other opportunities for influence (Lea & Young, 1984; Piven & Cloward, 1977), as well as the severe desperation associated with their condition.

If the L.A. rebellion is any indication, this condition exists today for many people in poverty. The widespread availability of guns is an additional factor in today's society which may influence the occurrence of violence. It is not only the access to guns which could encourage violence, but also the fact that inner-city youth have been socialized within a context of violence. These youth have had to contend with the constant reality or threat of violence in their own lives, and many have resorted to it themselves either as a means for survival or for manifesting power. Violence is not an extraordinary phenomenon for inner-city residents, as it is for many in more privileged classes. Given these conditions, in the context of spontaneous protest it should not be surprising that violence could emerge as a natural response.

Whatever the root causes of violent protest, the fact remains that it is unlikely to generate ongoing widespread public support. The form of protest that would probably generate the highest level of support involves coordinated actions of disruption. The Southern Civil Rights Movement serves as a relatively recent example of the potential successes of such strategies. Bus boycotts, sit-ins, and freedom rides, were coordinated actions which served to disrupt normal institutional functioning in the South, as well as generate public support in the North.

Similar kinds of actions today could perhaps have similar effects. For example, two protest strategies used by Unions of the Homeless, Welfare Rights Unions, and Up and Out of Poverty Now, involve taking over government-owned abandoned housing and constructing tent cities. These actions could be very successful strategies within the context of a widespread protest movement because they create disturbances which would usually force a response from policy-makers and they have the possibility of generating public support. The actions would potentially generate public support because of their nonviolent nature and because they provide a clear illustration of the protesters' grievances. Similar to how sit-ins in the Civil Rights Movement vividly illustrated the injustice of Southern segregation, housing takeovers and tent cities vividly illustrate the injustice of being deprived of housing. The association between the protesters' actions and their lack of housing is clear.

The potential effectiveness of such strategies is at times revealed by the responses from oppositional forces. When Up and Out of Poverty Now constructed a tent city in front of the state capitol building in Michigan in the winter of 1991-92, the conservative governor responded by propagating the false information that the protesters were not really homeless, but rather paid activists. This response revealed the administration's concern that the protest--by illustrating the hardship of living without housing--could serve to generate public support.

Another consideration in potential successes of protest strategies is how severe a disturbance the action creates for powerful groups. Actions which disrupt institutions of great importance to elite classes will generally be more effective strategies because they limit the ability of policy-makers to simply ignore the disturbances (Piven & Cloward, 1977). The construction of a tent city in front of Michigan's capitol building is an example of such a strategy. While the governor attempted to ignore the protest in the beginning, ultimately his administration was forced to confront the protesters and disband the tent city. Had the tent city been constructed in a remote area, it would not have created the same urgency for response.

In the context of a widespread poor people's movement, policy-makers may make more concerted efforts to withhold action, presenting protesters with the task of creating disturbances even more disruptive to elites. Taking over abandoned government-owned housing, for example, may no longer provoke a response if the property has relatively little value to the government and especially if it is located in remote areas. For protest to be effective under these conditions, bolder strategies would need to be devised. Taking over government office buildings might be an alternative strategy which would force a response from policy-makers. If such a protest strategy were sustained over a period of time, as similar strategies were in the Civil Rights Movement, policy-makers would be forced to take action. If physical repression were not an option due to public support, and protest leaders refused to be co-opted by elites, authorities would need an alternative response to the problem--either making room in prisons to contain the protesters or conceding to demands to create affordable housing.

The success of a protest movement can be measured in large part by the concessions made by policy-makers. Government concessions, however, are an extremely rare and extraordinary occurrence. The natural allegiance of policy-makers is to more powerful groups in their constituencies, whose interests often inherently contradict those of oppressed groups. Policy-makers will break these ties with elite classes only when protest threatens to undermine their own power (Piven & Cloward, 1977).

Even when concessions are granted, they usually include the absolute minimum necessary to appease the protesters and suppress the movement. This raises the danger for protesters that the concessions will fall short of meeting their true demands. But as this becomes apparent, it is usually too late to revive the spirit of protest. The inevitability of the decline of a protest movement suggests that protesters should maximize potential gains during those rare periods of mass upheaval and defiance by attempting to sustain disruption until meaningful concessions are offered (Piven & Cloward, 1977).

The potential success of a Homeless and Poor People's Movement, therefore, would be partially determined by the protesters' ability to sustain mass disruption and refuse the appeasements of policy-makers. For example, for homeless protesters to make the greatest gains toward alleviating homelessness, they would continue their housing and building takeovers and their construction of tent cities until meaningful housing legislation was passed. They would not be appeased by mere promises or proposals to rectify the problem, or by legislation to simply build more shelters or to provide housing for only special subgroups of the homeless population. They would continue their disruptive strategies until legislation was passed which would provide immediate and long-term programs for preserving and significantly expanding the low-cost housing supply.

Limitations on the Movement's Success

While a contemporary Homeless and Poor People's Movement could conceivably create some changes to benefit people in poverty, there are inherent limitations on the movement's potential success. Poor people's movements differ from many other social movements in that the goal is not equality. Poverty is not a solvable problem in a capitalist system. Short of a revolution, the most that people in poverty can expect from a successful protest movement is the attainment of some basic rights, such as access to food, housing, education, clean and safe environments, and health care.

While the elimination of poverty, therefore, is not a realistic goal of a poor people's movement, the alleviation of such specific problems as homelessness and hunger may be. Other possible goals of a' poor people's movement may not be as potentially attainable. Poor people's movements in general must contend with the vague nature of solutions to their grievances (Piven & Cloward, 1977). Since the root causes of poverty are impenetrable in a capitalist system, demands for reform to alleviate hardship are often somewhat abstract. Full employment, for example, is an impossibility within a strictly capitalist society due to fluctuations in market demand,[3] and strategies for attaining such an elusive goal are not straightforward.

It is more likely that goals of the movement which are relatively concrete and which pertain more to attainment of basic rights than to fundamental restructuring of the system, will be reached. But even some goals falling into this category may not be attainable without years or even decades of struggle. A struggle for widespread unionization of service workers, for example, could resemble to some extent the decades-long battle of the industrial labor movement. Over the past years, management has grown accustomed to its power over labor, so that any movement now to enhance the power of workers would undoubtedly create much disruption and chaos. The movement would strike at the heart of capitalist profitmaking-- minimization of labor costs. While unionized labor is not incompatible with a capitalist system, it often takes sustained, intense struggle to force concessions which so directly attack the interests of corporate elites.

In addition to requiring long-term struggles in this country, many contemporary issues of injustice are also contingent upon the struggles of impoverished and working classes throughout the world. The advent of global capitalism has created this dynamic scenario. The ability of corporations to transfer manufacturing plants from one country to another significantly undermines the power of industrial labor in every country. A resolution to this power imbalance will probably require worldwide unionization of industrial workers. While some efforts toward international unionization are currently underway (McGinn & Moody, 1993), this will undoubtedly be a difficult and long-term struggle, especially in Third World countries where efforts to unionize are often vehemently repressed by governments and multinational corporations.

The global nature of exploitation by multinational corporations will require that poor people's movements also adopt a global perspective in their struggles. This is by no means a new idea. For example, decades ago Malcolm X called for African American people to recognize their sisterhood and brotherhood with people of color in Third World nations. While there have been some efforts toward coalition-building across national boundaries, future movements by all oppressed people could be greatly enhanced by continued efforts in this area. Lack of resources, of course, could limit the effectiveness of such cross-national coalition-building strategies, but even efforts to further the awareness of the collective nature of oppressed people's struggles can help in creating a greater sense of solidarity and in resisting efforts by government to undermine protest by calling for patriotism or nationalism.

Global capitalism will by its nature create havoc for oppressed people throughout the world. The building of more just societies would ultimately require some dramatic restructuring of political systems. Free-market socialism has been suggested as a system of government to be strived for in the ensuing struggles for justice. A basic tenet of free-market socialism is that an individual's accumulation of wealth is limited to the extent that it deprives others of a minimal and humane share of the created wealth. It is a system which does not attempt to rid society of all privilege and inequality, yet strives for the eradication of social subjugation and for the establishment of justice (Barak, 1991).

Such political changes, if they ever occur, are still very distant. A contemporary Homeless and Poor People's Movement alone could not hope to accomplish such monumental goals. As discussed previously, the most that a successful movement could produce is the attainment of some basic rights for people in poverty, such as the right to housing. But the successful attainment of even these most basic rights would be a tremendous victory for impoverished people.

Notes

[1]These educational programs obviously were not designed only to serve the interests of low-income people, but middle income people as well.

[2]For a detailed discussion of the inadequacy of the federal poverty line, see the bibliography for Schwarz & Volgy (1992).

[3]It has in fact been argued that surplus labor is not simply a natural by-product of market operations, but a deliberate tactic by government to ease the flow of labor and undermine the bargaining power of workers (Piven & Cloward, 1971). Maintaining a labor surplus is accomplished through such strategies as slowing the rate of economic growth by restricting the money supply.

Chapter 4

Protest as the Means to End Homelessness

As outlined in the previous chapter, the emergence of a widespread Homeless and Poor People's Movement is by no means a certainty; and if one does emerge, the forms of protest which may occur and their potentials for success are also uncertain. Even though there are many uncertainties associated with the development of a protest movement, a movement is the best, and perhaps the only, hope for substantially alleviating the homelessness problem.

History has shown that steps toward greater equality and justice are not willingly conceded by political elites, but are forced by uprisings of oppressed people. The natural allegiance of political elites is to their powerful constituencies, and these ties are broken only when their own power is threatened by political instability (Piven & Cloward, 1977). Franklin Roosevelt's New Deal programs were forced by mass uprisings by industrial workers and the unemployed in the 1930's, and in order to enact these programs Roosevelt needed to undermine the interests of the business community. Similarly, federal efforts to desegregate the south in the 1960's were forced by uprisings of African Americans, and in order to support the protesters, John Kennedy needed to undermine the interests of southern economic and political elites (Piven & Cloward, 1977).

The role of protest in creating social change is often forgotten in historical hindsight. Roosevelt and Kennedy are remembered, and often glorified, for their controversial yet progressive roles in creating change to benefit oppressed people. The fact that massive protest movements were needed to force the concessions is often overlooked.

This selective historical memory may partially explain why many people are now looking to Clinton to willingly create dramatic progressive change. As discussed in the previous chapter, given Clinton's moderate political background, as well as the reality of U.S. politics, such hopes are likely to be violated. Clinton's self-description as a new kind of Democrat, which opposes much liberal philosophy and supports the interests of big business, will work against his willing enactment of sweeping progressive policies. In addition, the reality of power dynamics in the U.S. political system will work against it. The more progressive Clinton's policy initiatives are, the more likely it is that he will face resistance from other political and economic elites.

Such a scenario has been the case throughout U.S. history, but it is perhaps an even more serious obstacle today because previous restraints on the power of some elite groups are becoming obsolete. Laws to protect industrial workers, for example, have become outdated due to advances in technology which have allowed corporations to move production sites from one country or region to another. And unless substantial revisions are made to the North American Free Trade Agreement (NAFTA) and the global free trade proposals under the General Agreement on Tariffs and Trade (GATT), ratification of the agreements will give corporations virtually unrestrained power by granting them greater capital mobility and by allowing them to overturn any national laws deemed to be "trade restrictive" or "trade distorting" (Dawkins & Muffett, 1993). As described in the previous chapter, reclaiming a degree of government control over corporations in today's world would require that governments work together to establish new global regulations on multinationals to ensure protection of workers, consumers, and the environment.

In addition to this unrestrained power of big business, others in elite classes have now grown accustomed to government-bestowed privileges, making it that much more difficult to demand sacrifices from these groups. The "Reagan Revolution" resulted in many economic and political gains for the privileged classes, so that any efforts now to even restore the wealth and power imbalances to previous levels would be seen as threats to their interests.

In light of these political and economic realities, it is clear that one policy-maker or even several, regardless of rank or status, could not implement sweeping progressive policies on their own. As in previous eras, there is a need to bring pressure on policy-makers as a group as a means for creating progressive change. Without the pressure of mass protests in previous eras and the widespread public support that they generated, neither Roosevelt nor Kennedy would have been able to initiate progressive policies--even if they had wanted to. Today, Clinton cannot be expected to willingly initiate sweeping progressive policies which would establish a more equal and just society. The most that can be expected from him in realistic terms (in addition to the implementation of some modest proposals to alleviate hardship, particularly among the middle classes and impoverished children), is that he respond in a similar manner as these previous Democratic presidents if widespread protest does emerge--by choosing in the end to break his natural ties with powerful groups and instead side with the oppressed.

The Role of Outsiders in the Movement

The political nature of homelessness and poverty attests to the fact that professionals and other "outsiders" are inherently limited in bringing an end to homelessness. In order to generate sufficient pressure on policy-makers to get them to represent the interests of people in poverty, a mobilization of impoverished people will likely be necessary. Advocacy by itself in unlikely to generate sufficient pressure. Just as advocates for industrial workers and the unemployed in the 1930's would not have produced the changes brought about by the Labor Movement and the unemployed workers movement, and white advocates in the 1960's would not have produced the changes brought about by the Civil Rights Movement, advocates for homeless and poor people today will not be able to bring about the changes necessary to end homelessness. And while it can be argued that building a widespread protest movement among homeless and poor people would be difficult, the fact remains that it is perhaps the only possible solution to the problem.

The most meaningful role that professionals and other outsiders can play in helping to end homelessness is to act in ways that support the further development and strengthening of the movement. But before professionals and others are able to genuinely support the movement, many of us involved in homelessness and poverty issues must come to recognize the roles we currently play in the institutions which have arisen around the homelessness problem, and the extent to which these roles have served the interests of the establishment and not those of people who are homeless and living in poverty.

This is a particular concern for those of us involved in studying homelessness and poverty. Researchers who conduct victim-blaming research serve as the most extreme example of professionals acting in ways which serve the establishment. Victim-blaming research diverts attention from the structural sources of social problems by attributing blame to "deficiencies" in the people victimized by those problems (Ryan, 1971). Findings from such research benefit those in elite classes by providing a justification for inequality and therefore an excuse for inaction.

While relatively few researchers today conduct blatantly victim-blaming studies, many others also do a disservice to homeless people by continuing to focus on "deviant" characteristics of individual homeless people. What distinguishes these studies from victim-blaming ones is that they do not explicitly state that these individual characteristics are the cause of homelessness. By focusing on such issues as mental illness and substance abuse, however, there is still an implicit assumption that the homelessness problem can be traced to weaknesses in homeless people.

It is understandable that many researchers conduct such studies, because they are precisely the kind for which substantial funding can be obtained. A major source of funding for homelessness research, for example, is the federal agency, the National Institute of Mental Health. Restricting funding eligibility to certain kinds of studies is one way that government granting agencies serve to regulate the institution of homelessness research and direct its efforts toward preserving the interests of elite groups.

There have been, of course, many other researchers who have worked against the victim-blaming tradition by conducting studies which focus on the structural causes of homelessness and poverty. Indeed, it was the work of many of these researchers which was used to construct the analysis provided in Chapter Two of this book. The research institution which has arisen around the homelessness problem, therefore, has diverse components, but it is important for individual researchers to be aware of their roles in the institution and the fact that the institution has often worked in ways which serve the interests of elite classes.

The institution of charitable work and service provision surrounding homelessness and poverty has also at times worked inadvertently to serve the interests of elite groups. The institution has often served to mask structural sources of inequality and suffering, and instead focus public attention on private forms of charitable giving as the "solution" to the problems. Private charities, for example, represent the action of choice for conservatives. Former President Bush's call for "1000 points of light" to address problems of poverty and inequality is an example of how conservatives use the institution of charitable work to divert attention away from structural causes of social problems.

While conservatives tend to oppose any form of public programs to address issues of oppression and inequality, the kinds that they most willingly agree to are ones which focus on the symptoms rather than the causes of social problems. For example, Republicans (and even many Democrats today) are much more willing to support the use of public funds to build shelters for homeless people, rather than permanent housing. While shelters are needed as an immediate response to homelessness, they can by no means be seen as a productive long-term solution to the problem.

Given that charitable work and service provision are currently some of the few forms of relief available to homeless and poor people, the work of these groups should not be criticized. The point being made is that charity and service provision are not enough. Many people involved in the field recognize its limitations, and these people could contribute to long-term solutions by using their connections and influence to raise the public's awareness about the political nature of poverty. Charitable and service organizations often receive the bulk of public attention and media exposure, providing them with unique opportunities for influencing public opinion. Neglecting to portray poverty as a political issue only reinforces the public's perception that charity is the solution.

The institution surrounding the field of political advocacy on behalf of homeless people is very different from those surrounding homelessness research and charitable and service work. This institution as a whole tends to be more progressive and has certainly been more politically-oriented. This is perhaps best exemplified by the work of such national groups as the National Coalition for the Homeless, the National Law Center on Homelessness and Poverty, and the Community for Creative Non-Violence. These organizations have worked to raise the awareness of the public about the structural causes of homelessness and the politics of the issue, and have lobbied policy-makers and represented the legal interests of homeless people in an attempt to force government to take action.

While the work of these national groups, as well as similar local and state groups, has indeed been meaningful, the limits of advocacy in solving homelessness must be recognized. Given these limitations, the work of advocates could perhaps be strengthened if the groups worked more closely with grassroots protest organizations and followed their agenda for creating change.

Chris Sprowal, the founder of the first Union of the Homeless, has pointed out a fundamental difference in strategy between homeless protesters and professional advocates. In discussing the issue of immediate *vs.* long-term solutions, he noted that advocates are much more willing to make compromises with policy-makers, while homeless protesters demand immediate change. He attributed this difference in strategy to the fact that homeless people do not have the luxury of waiting for change because their survival is at stake (McMullen, 1988). Diane Bernard, the chairperson of the Michigan chapter of Up and Out of Poverty Now, has argued that professional advocates can at times actually obstruct the movement for change by assuming that they know best what needs to be done. She suggested that if advocates experience any contradiction between their own agenda and that of Up and Out of Poverty Now, they consider whose side their actions are truly benefitting (Bernard, 1992).

The remainder of this chapter is devoted to suggesting ways for professionals and other outsiders to support and encourage the mobilization of homeless and poor people. Fostering the empowerment of people in poverty is suggested as a guiding strategy toward accomplishing this goal. After defining the concept of empowerment and its basic principles, some concrete actions to support the movement are outlined.

The Concept of Empowerment

The term "empowerment" has been used to describe such a broad array of programs and policies that its meaning is no longer clear. In many ways, the term has been severely exploited. Professionals and politicians have attached the word to their ideas and programs because of its positive connotations. Former Vice President Quayle's use of the term during the 1992 Republican Convention to describe his administration's values and policies is a clear reflection of how over-used and exploited the word has become.

A distinction that can help clarify the term involves the target of change it implies. Some uses of the term reflect a conceptualization of empowerment as a process of helping people better adapt to existing social conditions. Teaching skills to people to help them find housing is an example of this definition of empowerment. The fault in this conceptualization is that the focus of change is on the people themselves--not on the oppressive structural conditions which are at the root of their problems. Changing the characteristics of people victimized by social problems will have little effect if the structural sources of the problems are not addressed.

An alternative conceptualization defines empowerment as a process of people banding together to challenge oppressive social conditions and to pressure policy-makers to create the necessary changes. This conceptualization, which is the one used in this book, can be termed "structural change empowerment" because the focus of change is the social structure itself. Structural change empowerment is both a personal and political process--it involves individual-, group-, and societal-level changes which lead to and include the mobilization of oppressed people.

Principles for Fostering Empowerment

There are several basic principles for fostering a structural change empowerment process. The most fundamental principle is supporting members of the oppressed group as leaders and decision-makers in the movement for change (Freire, 1970; Hall, 1981). In order to adhere to this principle, professionals must be willing to challenge and overcome the "expert" mentality that leads many of us to think that we know best what people need. We have been indoctrinated with this mentality through our education and professional experiences, and it is our task to disindoctrinate ourselves from this myth and come to understand that this mentality itself is oppressive and disempowering. We must instead foster a personal appreciation for cultural diversity and learn to have absolute respect for the people with whom we work.

This issue of a superior or condescending mentality pertains not only to professionals, but to a great extent to members of privileged classes in general. People in higher-income classes (particularly those of European descent) often have negative opinions and ideas regarding people in low-income classes (especially toward African Americans and other people of color). These beliefs reflect the racism and classism--albeit often subtle--which pervades our society, as well as the severe lack of appreciation for cultural diversity. Racism and classism are now particularly acute following the reign of right-wing presidents who encouraged such attitudes and beliefs. It is no wonder that the idea of oppressed groups leading a movement for progressive change sounds strange to many people in more privileged classes. But for those concerned about oppression, it is imperative that they trace these beliefs to their personal experiences of indoctrination and choose to challenge and overcome them.

A second basic principle for fostering empowerment involves respecting the abilities and skills of the oppressed group and supporting their further development. One means for adhering to this principle involves encouraging the collective generation of knowledge. This takes place through a dialogic method (Freire, 1970) in which people learn by communicating and problem-solving together. This process has been referred to as the creation of popular or common knowledge, in contrast to "expert" knowledge (Hall, 1981). An integral part of this process is a belief in the knowledge-creating capabilities of ordinary people. For this process to take place, people must challenge the dominant ideology which trivializes ordinary people's knowledge.

While the knowledge-creating abilities of people is the focus of an empowerment strategy, professionals can help facilitate this process by sharing their knowledge. In our society, knowledge is being increasingly concentrated in the hands of "experts" and the elite classes they often represent (Darcy de Oliveira & Darcy de Oliveira, 1975; Fals-Borda, 1982; Hall, 1979; Tandon, 1981). Empowerment of people can be facilitated by attempting to decentralize knowledge and the power it contains by putting knowledge in the hands of the oppressed (Hall, 1979; Tandon, 1981).

A third principle for fostering empowerment, which is related to the knowledge-generation process, involves an effort to develop a critical awareness about society, oppression, and history (Freire, 1970). Critical awareness can be defined as an ability to examine issues from a political perspective--to see the connections between the personal problems of individuals and the larger social structure (Freire, 1970). An essential part of the development of critical awareness is the process of "disindoctrination" (Vio Grossi, 1981). As described in a previous chapter, oppressed people have been indoctrinated with the dominant ideology, which justifies their oppression and blames them for their problems instead of the system. This happens through a process Freire (1970) called the "doctrine of personal culpability," an ideological schema which encourages and predisposes people to interpret their failures as evidence of personal deficit.

Development of critical awareness allows people to unmask the myths propagated by ideology which serve to keep people docile and self-blaming. Once such a developmental process begins, there is also the opportunity for increasing group cohesion and solidarity. Perceptions of inferiority and feelings of self-blame work to keep people divided; once these myths are dispelled, there is potential for oppressed people to unite in political action.

Development of critical awareness is an essential part of an empowerment strategy not only for people in the oppressed group, but also for the professionals and other outsiders involved, and for the public in general. Development of critical awareness on the part of outsiders involved in the movement enhances their abilities and desires to sacrifice their own power in order to promote the empowerment of the oppressed group. Development of critical awareness in the general public is also necessary in order to generate widespread support for the movement. Members of the public must come to understand the political nature of inequality and oppression if they are to support the movement.

A fourth principle for fostering empowerment is to encourage and support social action by the oppressed group. Social action is an integral component of the empowerment process because it is the force that can lead to structural change. While actual structural change may be a long-term goal, the process of social action can provide learning and growing experiences in itself. As Freire (1970) has stated, meaningful learning takes place through a process of praxis, a circular relationship of action and reflection. Social action taken by the people provides rich, broad learning experiences; the knowledge gained from the experiences may build strength for further social action.

The following section provides some concrete suggestions for supporting the development and strengthening of the Homeless and Poor People's Movement, based on these principles for fostering empowerment.

Supporting the Mobilization of Homeless and Poor People

Supporting homeless and poor people in their rightful and necessary role as leaders of the movement to end homelessness requires not only that we involve homeless people in our efforts to solve the problem, but that we allow them to be the decision-makers.

A fundamental aspect of supporting the mobilization of homeless and poor people, therefore, is a willingness to sacrifice our own power in order to support their empowerment. Diane Bernard, the chairperson of the Michigan chapter of Up and Out of Poverty Now, has in fact directly advised professional advocates to let the victims of poverty lead the movement for change, since they are the ones who best understand what action needs to be taken (Bernard, 1992).

Once professionals and others come to see homeless and poor people as the necessary leaders of the movement, the challenge then becomes developing specific strategies for encouraging their leadership. Some of the more obvious strategies might include inviting homeless and low-income people to serve on governing boards, and arranging for them to speak at public demonstrations or testify before legislature hearings. To their credit, some advocacy organizations have already begun incorporating these strategies into their organizations.

There remains an issue, however, of how integral a role these low-income participants play in the organizations. If only one or several are involved, it is possible that these participants would end up constituting a silent or passive minority. This is especially likely to be the case if active efforts are not made within the organizations to promote the role of these participants as decision-makers. As discussed above, people in poverty have been indoctrinated to blame themselves for their condition and to defer to "experts," and many professionals have been indoctrinated to believe that their knowledge and ideas are superior to those of "non-certified" ordinary people. Without concerted efforts to break these patterns, it is possible that they will continue to be played out within the organizations.

Given that the most meaningful form of protest for impoverished groups involves mass disruption rather than conventional political activities (Piven & Cloward, 1977), perhaps the most important role outsiders can take is to support and encourage direct action of people in poverty. Protest organizations comprised of homeless and poor people, such as Unions of the Homeless, Welfare Rights Unions, and Up and Out of Poverty Now, currently exist in cities across the country. Outsiders can support the strengthening of these groups through financial contributions, as well as personal involvement. (See the appendix for contact information for the groups). Indeed, progressive-minded people may want to consider donating time and resources to these grassroots protest organizations instead of (or in addition to) other more traditional forms of charity. In the long-term, this could be a better "investment" of resources because these groups address the root causes of the problem, not just its symptoms.

Because most of our efforts should be on supporting the direct action of homeless and poor people, we should not only invite members of these grassroots organizations to participate in our activities, but should offer to participate in theirs. It is likely that these groups would welcome outsider involvement in such activities as public demonstrations, because of the importance of sheer numbers and the display of broad-based support. In addition, these groups may welcome the sharing of resources, such as means of transportation and access to information. Diane Bernard has in fact suggested that an appropriate role for professionals is providing resources to the movement (Bernard, 1992). Sharing of personal expertise in such areas as legal matters may be particularly welcomed by these groups. A major activity of national advocacy groups has been providing legal representation to homeless people in an effort to force political change. For example, recent efforts have been directed toward promoting the right of homeless people to vote. Offering personal or organizational expertise such as this to grassroots organizations is an example of how professionals can work in conjunction with these groups in ways that promote the leadership of homeless and poor people and allow them to determine the course of action.

In cities where grassroots protest organizations do not exist, professionals and others can be involved in supporting their formation. Leona Smith, the president of the National Union of the Homeless (located in Philadelphia), has suggested that people interested in forming local unions contact the national office for information about the organization and its bylaws, as well as strategies for organizing. (See the appendix for contact information). Representatives from the national union sometimes travel to various cities to organize local chapters, depending on the availability of funding. Since homeless and low-income people themselves are likely to have more success at organizing unions, it would be ideal for individuals or organizations to raise funding to bring national representatives to their cities. Contacting other unions in their region for their advise and assistance would also help facilitate organizing efforts. Ms. Smith explained that it is important for all newly-formed chapters to be well-connected with the national office in order to maintain the integrity of individual chapters and to unite all chapters in national protest actions.

I was personally involved in helping form and sustain a local union in Lansing, Michigan, and the experience served as a powerful confirmation of my belief that homeless and low-income people are the appropriate leaders in the movement to end homelessness. I began my efforts by meeting with Wayne Pippin, president of the Detroit/Wayne County Union of the Homeless, to obtain more information about the union movement. (If I were to initiate such a project again, I would also contact the national office--as suggested above--and attempt to raise funds to bring their representatives to the city). In the summer of 1990, I approached homeless individuals with the idea of forming a union and quickly found some interested people. Following an initial period of developing some basic structure, union members became involved in a wide variety of social action activities. The union is currently a viable organization, comprised entirely of homeless and formerly-homeless people. According to Felida Smith, the director of the Lansing union, the union now has over 350 members.

The principles for fostering empowerment outlined above were incorporated into my efforts from the very beginning, and I believe that the success of the project can be partially attributed to that. The most fundamental principle for outsiders involved in forming unions is the promotion of homeless and low-income people as decision-makers and leaders. The need for outsiders to disindoctrinate themselves from an "expert" mentality is especially critical for those involved in such organizing efforts. Such efforts are not likely to succeed if outsiders are not willing or able to sacrifice their own power to promote the empowerment of others.

Encouraging the development and strengthening of grassroots organizations of homeless and poor people is perhaps the most significant action that we, as outsiders, can take to support the movement. Within the context of such organizations, all the principles for fostering empowerment naturally exist. By their nature, the groups support the leadership role of homeless and poor people, collective forms of problem-solving, the development of critical awareness and group cohesion, and the implementation of social action.

Genuinely supporting the mobilization of homeless and poor people also includes a willingness to not be involved in certain aspects of the movement if these grassroots organizations deem that appropriate. Leaders may decide, for example, that they want certain activities, such as meetings or public relations, reserved for homeless and low-income people only. A similar situation exists today in groups working for advancing the rights of other oppressed groups, such as African Americans and women. While most African American groups desire the support of Anglos, and most women's groups desire the support of men, they generally do not choose to have them as spokespersons for their groups. Indeed, there was a time in the Civil Rights Movement when leaders decided to ban the involvement of Anglos from certain activities because it was impeding the leadership development of African Americans (Freeman, 1983). Outsiders involved in the Homeless and Poor People's Movement must be aware of similar possibilities concerning their involvement and be willing to abide by the directives of movement leaders.

A related issue for outsiders concerns the selection of protest strategies. In our efforts to support the movement, we must guard against any desires we may have to channel protest activities into conventional political realms. As discussed in the previous chapter, impoverished groups exert their greatest influence through disruptive actions, and opportunities for meaningful protest are often wasted by efforts to divert energy into building formal organizations (Piven & Cloward, 1977). Many outsiders may have difficulty accepting mass disruption as an appropriate strategy (as revealed by the controversy created by Piven & Cloward's book), especially if such tactics would become widespread. Regardless of one's personal opinion about militancy or disruption, it is absolutely inappropriate for outsiders to attempt to channel insurgency into forms of protest which they may consider to be more ethically correct.

The issue here concerns not only violence, but even nonviolent mass disruption. Many people, especially those in more privileged classes, tend to favor consensus-building strategies over confrontational ones. The crucial point for these people to consider is that consensus-building is usually only an effective strategy for members of more privileged groups. Members of impoverished groups have virtually no potential for influence through such strategies. Their lack of resources makes "dissensus" strategies the only viable option for creating meaningful change (Piven & Cloward, 1992).

Violence is a separate issue from mass disruption. As illustrated by the Civil Rights Movement, it is possible for disruption to be carried out through civil disobedience tactics. But as discussed in the previous chapter, the potential for such coordinated actions depends to a great extent upon the level of group solidarity that can be achieved before unrest reaches the point of widespread protest.

It is likely that most participants in a coordinated protest movement would oppose outbreaks of violence, not only on moral grounds and because it would be primarily other low-income people who would suffer, but also for strategic and personal survival reasons. People who live in poverty are acutely aware of the potential for repression by authorities. It is a basic characteristic of life for many of them. Most movement participants would likely oppose violence because it gives authorities a justification for repression and counter-violence.

But if violence would occur in the context of protest, it would be an issue for protest leaders to address, not outsiders involved in the movement. People from more privileged groups are in no position to judge or try to direct the actions of people in poverty, although they often assume they are due to racist and classist indoctrination. Reaction to the L.A. rebellion in the spring of 1992 serves as a useful example. Many observers, especially conservatives, readily judged the actions of rioters and looters and chastised them for their "immoral" behavior. Such responses serve the interests of the conservative perspective by blaming the outbreak on "deficiencies" in impoverished people, thereby diverting attention from the root causes of the protest. While it is important not to glorify the actions of the L.A. protesters--especially because it was primarily other low-income and racially oppressed groups who were hurt by the insurgency--it is vitally important to trace the disruption to its root, structural causes. One does not need to condone violence in order to abstain from judging oppressed people who commit such acts. If anyone is to blame, it is the government which allowed and encouraged the violence-breeding conditions of devastating poverty and institutionalized racism to exist.

Similarly, outsiders attempting to support the mobilization of homeless and poor people would have no right to judge the actions of protesters--whatever they may be--or to try to discourage certain forms of protest. This issue of potentially-controversial protest strategies exemplifies how critical it is to support homeless and poor people in their rightful role as leaders in the movement. If an outsider genuinely believed in the appropriateness and necessity of homeless and poor people leading the movement, such an issue would not arise.

In addition to supporting the direct action of homeless protesters, professionals and others can serve the cause of the movement by engaging in strategies which promote the development of critical awareness within their own professional and personal circles. Gans (1992) has suggested, for example, that those who speak on behalf of the poor should initiate an intellectual and cultural defense of people in poverty in reaction to the "war against the poor." While it is ideal to allow people in poverty to represent themselves in this defense whenever possible, it is also appropriate for others to engage in consciousness-raising strategies to illustrate broad-based support for such progressive ideas. Any strategies which heighten awareness about the political nature of homelessness and poverty, and dispute victim-blaming ideas and conservative justifications for the problems, would serve the movement's goals.

Many professionals have access to various "audiences" which would provide such opportunities for influence. Professors and teachers have a particularly useful opportunity because of their access to students. Others have such opportunities at conferences or community meetings, and with colleagues and friends. Journal and magazine articles offer an additional opportunity for many professionals to promote progressive ideas and actions.

Professionals interested in engaging in such consciousness-raising strategies could perhaps strengthen their efforts by contacting grassroots protest organizations for their advise and educational materials. For example, the National Union of the Homeless has a video documenting their nationwide series of takeovers of government-owned abandoned housing. This video, called "Takeover," can be purchased from the national office. (See the appendix for contact information).

Conclusion

The point of this chapter has been to suggest ways for professionals and other outsiders to support the mobilization of homeless and poor people. Those of us who are concerned about bringing an end to homelessness cannot necessarily assume that the actions we are taking are ultimately productive. Part of supporting the movement is learning to challenge our assumptions about our roles in bringing an end to the problem. Adhering to empowerment principles, in particular promoting the leadership of homeless and poor people and developing a willingness to sacrifice our own power, allows us to be more confident that the actions we are taking are indeed productive.

The emergence of a widespread Homeless and Poor People's Movement is by no means contingent upon the work of professionals or other outsiders. If conditions are right, the movement will occur, regardless of the actions of outsiders. This is the way it has always been. In a process that continues to defy understanding, various forces at times combine to bring oppressed people together in powerful movements for justice and social change. It is unknown whether current conditions will result in such a phenomenon, but it is likely that a resolution to the homelessness problem depends on it.

Appendix

National Union of the Homeless
246 Arch Street
Philadelphia, PA 19106
(215) 923-1694

National Up and Out of Poverty Now
13220 Woodward Avenue
Highland Park, MI 48203
(313) 868-3660

National Welfare Rights Union
13220 Woodward Avenue
Highland Park, MI 48203
(313) 868-3660

Lansing Area Homeless Persons Union
106 West Allegan Street, Suite 403
Lansing, MI 48933
(517) 372-1854

Detroit/Wayne County Union of the Homeless
3627 Cass Avenue
Detroit, MI 48201
(313) 831-1118

Bibliography

Chapter One

Piven, F. & Cloward, R. (1979). *Poor people's movements: Why they succeed, how they fail.* New York: Pantheon.

Chapter Two

Adams, C. (1986). Homelessness in the post-industrial city: Views from London and Philadelphia. *Urban Affairs Quarterly, 21*(4), 527-549.

American Public Welfare Association. (1989). Housing the poor. *Public Welfare, 47*(1), 5-12.

Apgar, W., DiPasquale, D., Cummings, J. & McArdle, N. (1990). *The State of the Nation's Housing 1990.* Cambridge, MA: Joint Center for Housing Studies of Harvard University.

Apgar, W. & Brown, J. (1988). *The State of the Nation's Housing.* Cambridge, MA: Joint Center for Housing Studies of Harvard University.

Barak, G. (1991). *Gimme shelter: A social history of homelessness in contemporary America.* New York: Praeger.

Barancik, S. (1989). *Poverty Rate and Household Income Stalemate as Rich-Poor Gap Hits Post-War High.* Washington, DC: Center on Budget and Policy Priorities.

Barlett, D. & Steele, J. (1992). *America: What went wrong?* Kansas City, MO: Andrews and McMeel.

Bassuk, E. & Lauriat, A. (1984). The politics of homelessness. In R. Lamb (Ed.), *The homeless mentally ill* (pp. 301-313). Washington DC: American Psychiatric Association.

Beauregard, R. (1988). *Alternatives: Gentrification, Strategic Initiatives, and the Left,* 4. New York: Analysis and Policy Press and the Institute for Democratic Socialism.

Belcher, J. & Singer, J. (1988). Homelessness: A cost of Capitalism. *Social Policy*, *18*(4), 44-48.

Bluestone, B. (1987). Deindustrialization and unemployment in America. In P. Staudohar and H. Brown (Eds.). *Deindustrialization and plant closure* (pp. 3-15). Lexington, MA: Lexington Books.

Bluestone, B. & Harrison, B. (1982). *The deindustrialization of America*. New York: Basic Books.

Boroughs, D., Hage, D., Collins, S. & Cohen, W. (1992, November 2). What's wrong with the American economy. *U.S. News & World Report*, *113*(17), 36-51.

Bywater, W. (1985). Imports and U.S. job loss--the color TV industry. In B. Lall (Ed.), *Economic dislocation and job loss* (pp. 31-39). Tallahassee, FL: Rose Printing Company.

Children's Defense Fund. (1989). *A Vision for America's Future*. Washington, DC.

Dawkins, K. & Muffett, W. (1993, January). The free-trade sellout. *The Progressive*, *57*(1), 18-20.

Dillingham, F., Geake, R., DiNello, G., Cropsey, H. & Cherry, J. (1987). *Housing in Michigan: Low-Income and Senior Citizen Families in Crisis*. Lansing, MI: Senate Human Resources and Senior Citizen Committee.

Dreier, P. (1987). Community-based housing: A progressive approach to a new federal policy. *Social Policy*, *18*(2), 18-22.

Feingold, S. (1984, February). Emerging careers: Occupations for post-industrial society. *The Futurist*, *18*(1), 9-16.

First, R., Roth, D. & Arewa, B. (1988). Homelessness: Understanding the dimensions of the problem for minorities. *Social Work*, *33*, 120-124.

Frank, A. (1972). The development of underdevelopment. In J. Cockcroft, A. Frank & D. Johnson (Eds.), *Dependence and underdevelopment: Latin America's political economy* (pp. 3-17). New York: Anchor Books.

Freeman, R. & Hall, B. (1987). Permanent homelessness in America? *Population Research and Policy Review*, *6*, 3-27.

Fuentes, A. & Ehrenreich, B. (1983). *Women in the global factory*. Boston: South End Press.

Greenstein, R. & Barancik, S. (1990). *Drifting Apart: New Findings on Growing Income Disparities Between the Rich, the Poor, and the Middle Class*. Washington, DC: Center on Budget and Policy Priorities.

Greenstein, R. & Jaeger, A. (1992). *Number in Poverty Hits 20-Year High as Recession Adds 2 Million More Poor, Analysis Finds*. Washington, DC: Center on Budget and Policy Priorities.

Hage, D. & Collins, S. (1993, February 22). Betting on Wall Street. *U.S. News & World Report*, *114*(7), 42-43.

Harrington, M. (1984). *The new American poverty*. New York: Holt, Rinehart and Winston.

Harris, C. (1987). Magnitude of job loss. In P. Staudohar and H. Brown (Eds.), *Deindustrialization and plant closure* (pp.89-100). Lexington, MA: Lexington Books.

Harrison, B. & Bluestone, B. (1990). Wage polarisation in the U.S. and the "flexibility" debate. *Cambridge Journal of Economics*, *14*, 351-373.

Harrison, B. & Bluestone, B. (1988). *The Great U-Turn: Corporate restructuring and the polarizing of America*. New York: Basic Books.

Hartman, C., Keating, D. & LeGates, R. (1982). *Displacement: How to fight it*. Berkeley, CA: National Housing Law Project.

Hopper, K. (1988). More than passing strange: Homelessness and mental illness in New York City. *American Ethnologist, 15,* 155-167.

Hopper, K., Susser, E. & Conover, S. (1985). Economies of makeshift: Deindustrialization and homelessness in New York City. *Urban Anthropology, 14*(1-3), 183-236.

Hutchinson, F., Lav, I. & Greenstein, R. (1992). *A Hand Up: How State Earned Income Credits Help Working Families Escape Poverty.* Washington, DC: Center on Budget and Policy Priorities.

Jaeger, A, Shapiro, I. & Greenstein, R. (1992). *New Census Report Shows Dramatic Rise Since 1979 in Workers with Low Earnings.* Washington, DC: Center on Budget and Policy Priorities.

Jonas, S. (1986). On homelessness and the American way. *American Journal of Public Health, 76*(9), 1084-1086.

Kasinitz, P. (1984). Gentrification and homelessness: The single room occupant and the inner city revival. *Urban and Social Change Review, 17*(1), 9-14.

Kuttner, R. (1983, July). The declining middle. *The Atlantic Monthly, 252*(1), 60-72.

Lav, I., Gold, S., Lazere, E. & Greenstein, R. (1993). *The States and the Poor: How Budget Decisions Affected Low Income People in 1992.* Washington, DC: Center on Budget and Policy Priorities. Albany, NY: Center for the Study of the States.

Leonard, P. & Lazere, E. (1992). *A Place to Call Home.* Washington, DC: Center on Budget and Policy Priorities.

Loewenstein, G. (1985). The new underclass: A contemporary sociological dilemma. *The Sociological Quarterly, 26*(1), 35-48.

Marcuse, P. (1988). Neutralizing homelessness. *Socialist Review*, *18*(1), 69-96.

Marotto, R. & Friedland, W. (1987). Streetpeople and community public policy in Santa Cruz, California. *Journal of Applied Sociology*, *4*, 71-87.

McChesney, K. (1990). Family homelessness: A systemic problem. *Journal of Social Issues*, *46*(4), 191-205.

Michigan League for Human Services. (1992, October). *Memo to Members*. Lansing, MI.

Moberg, D. (1993, March 22). The jobless recovery. *In These Times*, *17*(9), 25-27.

Moody, K. (1992a, October). Corporate America on the free trade deal: 'An extraordinarily good agreement.' *Labor Notes*, *163*, 1,9,15.

Moody, K. (1992b, October). The free trade deal: How it will affect trucking, auto, & communications. *Labor Notes*, *163*, 8-9.

Moore, C., Sink, D. & Hoban-Moore, P. (1988). The politics of homelessness. *Political Science and Politics*, *21*, 57-63.

National Coalition for the Homeless (1988, July). *Over the edge: Homeless families and the welfare system*. Washington, DC.

Phillips, K. (1992). *The politics of rich and poor: Wealth and the American electorate in the Reagan aftermath*. New York: HarperPerennial.

Redburn, F. & Buss, T. (1987). Beyond shelter: The homeless in the USA. *Cities*, *4*(1), 63-69.

Reich, R. (1991). *The work of nations*. New York: Vintage Books.

Reyes, L. & Waxman, L. (1989). *A Status Report on Hunger and Homelessness in America's Cities: 1989.* Washington, DC: U.S. Conference of Mayors.

Riessman, F. (1986). The language of the 80's: A new look at the homeless. *Social Policy, 16,* 2-10.

Ryan, W. (1971). *Blaming the victim.* New York: Vintage Press.

Samuel, H. (1985). Magnitude of the dislocation. In B. Lall (Ed.), *Economic dislocation and job loss* (pp. 11-13). Tallahassee, FL: Rose Printing Company.

Safety Network, (1988a, September). Hunger act to be signed by Reagan. Washington, DC: National Coalition for the Homeless, 1.

Safety Network, (1988b, September). Jobless Americans going without benefits. Washington, DC: National Coalition for the Homeless, 4.

Shapiro, I., Gold, S., Sheft, M., Strawn, J., Summer, L. & Greenstein, R. (1991). *The States and the Poor: How Budget Decisions in 1991 Affected Low Income People.* Washington, DC: Center on Budget and Policy Priorities. Albany, NY: Center for the Study of the States.

Shapiro, I. & Greenstein, R. (1988). *Holes in the Safety Nets: Poverty Programs and Policies in the States.* Washington, DC: Center on Budget and Policy Priorities.

Shapiro, I. & Nichols, M. (1992). *Far from Fixed: An Analysis of the Unemployment Insurance System.* Washington, DC: Center on Budget and Policy Priorities.

Shinn, M. (1992). Homelessness: What is a psychologist to do? *American Journal of Community Psychology, 20*(1), 1-24.

Snow, D., Baker, S. & Anderson, L. (1988). On the precariousness of measuring insanity in insane contexts. *Social Problems, 35*(2), 192-196.

Snow, D., Baker, S., Anderson, L. & Martin, M. (1986). The myth of pervasive mental illness among the homeless. *Social Problems, 33*(5), 407-423.

Staudohar, P. & Brown, H. (1987). *Deindustrialization and plant closure*. Lexington, MA: Lexington Books.

Stoner, M. (1983). The plight of homeless women. *Social Service Review, 57*(4), 565-581.

Thelwell, R. (1985). Governmental policies and effectively utilizing human resources. In B. Lall (Ed.) *Economic dislocation and job loss* (pp. 40-56). Tallahassee, FL: Rose Printing Company.

Toro, P. & Warren, M. (1991). Homelessness, psychology, and public policy. *American Psychologist, 46*(11), 1205-1207.

Uchitelle, L. (1993, March 28). Those high-tech jobs can cross the border, too. *New York Times, CXLII*(49,284), E4.

Waxman, L. & Frye, D. (1992). *A Status Report on Hunger and Homelessness in America's Cities: 1992*. Washington, DC: U.S. Conference of Mayors.

Weintraub, J. (1993, January). Citizens shut out. *The Progressive, 57*(1), 21.

Winpisinger, W. (1985). Technological tyranny--economic conversion. In B. Lall (Ed.), *Economic dislocation and job loss* (pp. 22-30). Tallahassee, FL: Rose Printing Company.

Wright, J. & Lam, J. (1987). Homelessness and the low-income housing supply. *Social Policy, 17*, 48-53.

Chapter Three

Apgar, W., DiPasquale, D., Cummings, J. & McArdle, N. (1990). *The State of the Nation's Housing 1990*. Cambridge, MA: Joint Center for Housing Studies of Harvard University.

Barak, G. (1991). *Gimme shelter: A social history of homelessness in contemporary America*. New York: Praeger.

Benyon, J. (1987). Interpretations of civil disorder. In J. Benyon & J. Solomos (Eds.), *The roots of urban unrest* (pp. 23-41). Oxford: Pergamon Press.

Bernard, D. (1992). *On hunger and the Up and Out of Poverty Now movement*. Detroit, MI: Michigan Up and Out of Poverty Now.

Boase, P. (1980). *The rhetoric of protest and reform: 1878-1898*. Athens, OH: Ohio University Press.

DeParle, J. (1992, December 20). Clinton social policy camps: Bill's vs. Hillary's. *New York Times, CXLII*(49,186), A1,12.

Epstein, B. (1990). Rethinking social movement theory. *Socialist Review, 20*(1), 35-66.

Freire, P. (1970). *Pedagogy of the oppressed*. New York: The Seabury Press.

Freeman, J. (1983). On the origins of social movements. In J. Freeman (Ed.), *Social movements of the Sixties and Seventies* (pp. 8-30). New York: Longman.

Gamson, W. (1990). *The strategy of social protest*. Belmont, CA: Wadsworth Publishing Company.

Gans, H. (1992). The war against the poor. *Dissent, 39*(4), 461-465.

Goldberg, R. (1991). *Grassroots resistance: Social movements in Twentieth Century America*. Belmont, CA: Wadsworth Publishing Company.

Greenhouse, S. (1993, February 20). Clinton's program gets endorsement of Fed's chairman. *New York Times, CXLII*(49,248), A1,6.

Greenstein, R. & Leonard, P. (1993). *A New Direction: The Clinton Budget and Economic Plan*. Washington, DC: Center on Budget and Policy Priorities.

Hopper, K., Susser, E. & Conover, S. (1985). Economies of makeshift: Deindustrialization and homelessness in New York City. *Urban Anthropology, 14*(1-3). 183-236.

Jenkins, C. (1983). Resource mobilization theory and the study of social movements. *Annual Review of Sociology, 9*, 527-553.

Kerbo, H. (1982). Movements of 'crisis' and movements of 'affluence.' *Journal of Conflict Resolution, 26*(4), 645-663.

Knoll, E., Rocawich, L., Conniff, R. & Buell, J. (1992, December). Four more years. *The Progressive, 56*(12), 8-11.

Korpi, W. (1974). Conflict, power, and relative deprivation. *The American Political Science Review, 68*(4), 1569-1578.

Kramer, M. (1993, January 26). National president, Up and Out of Poverty Now. Personal communication.

Kuttner, R. (1983, July). The declining middle. *The Atlantic Monthly, 252*(1), 60-72.

Lea, J. & Young, J. (1984). *What is to be done about law and order?* Middlesex, England: Penguin Books.

LeVeen, D. (1983). Organization or disruption? Strategic options for marginal groups: The case of the Chicago Indian Village. In J. Freeman (Ed.), *Social movements of the sixties and seventies* (pp. 211-234). New York: Longman.

McCammon, H. (1990). Legal limits on labor militancy: U.S. labor law and the right to strike since the New Deal. *Social Problems, 37*(2), 206-229.

McCarthy, J. & Zald, M. (1977). Resource mobilization and social movements: A partial theory. *American Journal of Sociology, 82*(6), 1212-1241.

McGinn, M. & Moody, K. (1993, March). Labor goes global. *The Progressive, 57*(3), 24-27.

Muwakkil, S. (1993, April 5). Ganging together. *In These Times, 17*(10), 14-18.

Nasar, S. (1992, December 27). Clinton job plan in manufacturing meets skepticism. *New York Times, CXLII*(49,193), A1,10.

National Law Center on Homelessness and Poverty (1993, March 1). Clinton economic package introduced. *In Just Times, 4*(3), 1-2.

Oberschall, A. (1973). *Social conflict and social movements*. Englewood Cliffs, NJ: Prentice-Hall.

Phillips, K. (1992). *The politics of rich and poor: Wealth and the American electorate in the Reagan aftermath*. New York: HarperPerennial.

Piven, F. & Cloward, R. (1992). Normalizing collective protest. In A. Morris & C. McClurg Mueller (Eds.), *Frontiers in social movement theory* (pp. 301-325). New Haven, CT: Yale University Press.

Piven, F. & Cloward, R. (1977). *Poor people's movements: Why they succeed, how they fail*. New York: Pantheon.

Piven, F. & Cloward, R. (1971). *Regulating the poor: The functions of public welfare*. New York: Pantheon.

Schwarz, J. & Volgy, T. (1992). *The forgotten Americans: Thirty million Americans working but poor*. New York: Norton.

Tilly, C., Tilly, L. & Tilly, R. (1975). *The rebellious century*. Cambridge, MA: Harvard University Press.

Vio Grossi, F. (1981). Socio-political implications of participatory research. *Convergence, 14*(3), 43-50.

Walsh, K., Cooper, M. & Robbins, C. (1992, December 28). Clinton: Doing it all. *U.S. News & World Report, 113*(25), 18-20.

Wilkins, R. (1992, November/December). White out. *Mother Jones, 17*(6), 44-48.

Chapter Four

Bernard, D. (1992). *On hunger and the Up and Out of Poverty Now movement*. Detroit, MI: Michigan Up and Out of Poverty Now.

Darcy de Oliveira, R. & Darcy de Oliveira, M. (1975). *The Militant Observer*. Geneva: Institut d'Action Culturelle (IDAC Document 9).

Dawkins, K. & Muffett, W. (1993, January). The free-trade sellout. *The Progressive, 57*(1), 18-20.

Fals-Borda, O. (1982). Participatory research and rural social change. *Journal of Rural Cooperation, 10*(1), 25-40.

Freeman, J. (1983). A model for analyzing the strategic options of social movement organizations. In J. Freeman (Ed.), *Social movements of the Sixties and Seventies* (pp. 193-210). New York: Longman.

Freire, P. (1970). *Pedagogy of the oppressed*. New York: The Seabury Press.

Gans, H. (1992). The war against the poor. *Dissent, 39*(4), 461-465.

Hall, B. (1979). Knowledge as a commodity and participatory research. *Prospects, 9*(4), 4-20.

Hall, B. (1981). Participatory research, popular knowledge, and power: A personal reflection. *Convergence, 14*(3), 6-17.

McMullen, M. (1988). Union of the Homeless: The rank and file of the streets. *The Tri-State Peace & Justice Journal, 3*(1), 3.

Piven, F. & Cloward, R. (1992). Normalizing collective protest. In A. Morris & C. McClurg Mueller (Eds.), *Frontiers in social movement theory* (pp. 301-325). New Haven, CT: Yale University Press.

Piven, F. & Cloward, R. (1977). *Poor people's movements: Why they succeed, how they fail*. New York: Pantheon.

Ryan, W. (1971). *Blaming the victim*. New York: Vintage Press.

Tandon, R. (1981). Participatory research in the empowerment of people. *Convergence, 24*(3), 20-29.

Vio Grossi, F. (1981). Socio-political implications of participatory research. *Convergence, 14*(3), 43-50.

Index

A

advocacy organizations, 2, 3, 67-68, 72, 73. *See also* professionals
AFDC. *See* Aid to Families with Dependent Children
African Americans, 8, 42, 49, 50, 53, 55, 61, 63, 69, 75
    among homeless. *See* homelessness, characteristics of
      victims
Aid to Families with Dependent Children (AFDC), 24
Alinsky, Saul, 55
Anglos, among homeless. *See* homelessness, characteristics of
    victims
Asian Americans, among homeless. *See* homelessness,
    characteristics of victims
automated production. *See* corporations

B

bankruptcies, corporations. *See* corporations
Bernard, Diane, 30, 68, 72, 73
billionaires, 8, 47
Bush, George, 18, 27, 34, 48, 67

C

capital mobility. *See* corporate flight
capitalism, 60, 61
    global, 18, 61
Carter, Jimmy, 18
charities, 66-67, 72
child labor regulations, 43
children among homeless. *See* homelessness, characteristics of
    victims
Civil Rights Movement, 53, 56, 58, 59, 63, 65, 75
classism, 69, 76

Clinton, Bill, 2, 3, 10, 11, 27, 34-44, 48, 49, 64, 65
    economic proposals, 35-37
    housing policy proposals, 38-39
    political background, 2, 3, 41-42, 64
    poverty policy proposals, 39-42
    tax policy proposals, 38
Community for Creative Nonviolence (CCNV), 67
consumer protection regulations, 10, 43, 64
corporate flight, 9-11, 33, 35, 36, 42-43, 48
corporations
    automated production, 9, 11, 33, 35, 42-43
    bankruptcies, 19, 47
    deregulation of, 18-19, 43
    downsizing, 9, 36, 41
    mergers, 19, 22
    plant closings, 12, 32, 33, 47
    takeovers, 19, 22
    See also multinational corporations
critical awareness, 70-71
cutbacks in social programs. *See* government spending

D

deindustrialization. *See* economic transformation
Democratic Leadership Council, 42
Department of Housing and Urban Development. *See* Housing
    and Urban Development
Detroit/Wayne County Union of the Homeless, 3, 74, 79
deregulation of business. *See* corporations
"devolution", 23, 24
"disindoctrination", 32, 70
downsizing, corporations. *See* corporations

E

Earned Income Tax Credit (EITC), 39, 40, 41
economic disparity, 1, 2, 7-8, 12-14, 26, 33, 43, 46, 47, 51. *See also*
    redistribution of wealth
economic growth, 13-14, 15

economic transformation, 1, 3, 4, 8-14, 31, 33, 36, 41, 50
electoral patterns, 49-50
employment. *See* jobs
employment among homeless. *See* homelessness, characteristics of
  victims
empowerment
    definition of, 68-69
    principles for fostering, 69-71, 74, 77-78
environmental protection regulations, 9, 10, 11, 43, 64

F

"fair market rent", 24
families among homeless. *See* homelessness, characteristics of
  victims
federal debt, 19, 22, 47, 48
Federal Reserve Board, 18, 37
Food Stamps, 24, 40
Free Market Socialism, 61-62
Freire, Paulo, 32, 70, 71

G

GA. *See* General Assistance
gap between rich and poor. *See* economic disparity
GATT. *See* General Agreement on Tariffs and Trade
General Agreement on Tariffs and Trade (GATT), 10-11, 43, 64
General Assistance (GA), relation to homelessness, 25
gentrification. *See* housing
GNP, 22
government spending
    increases in defense, 23
    federal cutbacks for housing, 23
    federal cutbacks for income support, 24
    state cutbacks, 24-25
grassroots organizations, 2, 29, 30, 50, 55, 68, 73, 74
Great Depression, 5, 19, 34
Great Society programs, 34
Greenspan, Alan, 37

Gross National Product. *See GNP*

H

Head Start, 39
Homeless and Poor Peoples Movement
    background on, 2, 3, 29-30
    factions of, 52-55
    limitations on, 60-62
    potential for widespread development, 3, 30-51
    potential forms of, 52-55
    potential successes of, 55-60
    protest strategies of, 30, 54-55, 58-60, 75
    ways of supporting, 65-68, 71-77
homelessness
    attempts to justify. *See* homelessness, government's response
        to
    causes of. *See* homelessness, structural causes of
    characteristics of victims, 6-7
    government's response to, 1, 5, 26-28
    political nature of, 1, 3, 4, 26, 77
    prevalence of, 5-6, 34, 51
    research on, 1, 66
    role of professionals in solving. *See* professionals
    structural causes of, 4, 7-26
housing
    displacement from, 16-17, 39
    gentrification, 15-17, 21
    historical patterns of, 14-15
    low-cost, diminishing supply of, 14-17, 33, 39, 47
    public housing, 23, 38, 39
    redlining, 16
    relation to deindustrialization, 14
    subsidies, 17, 23, 39
Housing Act of 1949, 23
Housing and Urban Development, 23, 39
housing takeovers, 30, 58, 59
HUD. *See* Housing and Urban Development

I

income. *See* jobs, wages
income disparity. *See* economic disparity
inequality. *See* economic disparity
inner cities, 44, 45, 49, 57

J

Jackson, Jessie, 49
jobs
 information sector, 9, 12
 lay-offs, 33, 34, 36
 manufacturing sector, 8-14, 33, 36-37, 45, 48, 54
 plant closings. *See* corporations
 service sector, 9, 11-13, 33, 36-37, 54
 wages, polarization of, 8, 12-14, 36-37, 48

K

Kennedy, John, 2, 49, 63, 65
King, Martin Luther, 52
Kramer, Marian, 29, 30

L

L.A. rebellion. *See* Los Angeles rebellion
labor movement
 contemporary, 54, 60-61
 of the 1930's and 1940's, 33, 34, 54, 56, 60, 65
labor protection regulations, 9, 10, 43, 64
labor unions
 declining power of, 13, 19, 43, 54
 proportion of U.S. workforce in, 13
Lansing Area Homeless Persons Union, 3, 74, 79
Latino Americans, 8, 49, 50
 among homeless. *See* homelessness, characteristics of victims
lay-offs. *See* jobs
Los Angeles rebellion, 2, 29, 45, 50, 52, 55, 57, 76

low-cost housing. *See* housing

M

Malcolm X, 53, 61
manufacturing jobs. *See* jobs
mental illness, 1, 26-27, 28, 66
mergers, corporate. *See* corporations
middle class, erosion of, 8, 12-14, 33, 51. *See also* social class
structure
millionaires, 8, 47
minimum wage, 24, 37, 43
minorities
    among homeless. *See* homelessness, characteristics of
      victims
    and the poverty rate. *See* poverty rate
multinational corporations, 9, 10, 11, 42-43, 61, 64

N

NAFTA. *See* North American Free Trade Agreement
National Coalition for the Homeless, 67
National Institute of Mental Health (NIMH), 66
National Law Center on Homelessness and Poverty, 39, 67
National Union of the Homeless, 3, 73, 77
Native Americans, 49, 50
    among homeless. *See* homelessness, characteristics of victims
New Deal, 57, 63
North American Free Trade Agreement (NAFTA), 10-11, 36, 43,
    64

P

Perot, Ross, 48
Pippin, Wayne, 74
plant closings, corporate. *See* corporations
polarization of wages. *See* jobs
political marginalization, 31, 56
poverty line, 24, 40

poverty rate, 8, 27
    for children, 8
    for minorities, 8
    for working families, 8
praxis, 71
professionals
    appropriate roles for, 3-4, 65-68, 72-77
    "expert" mentality of, 3-4, 69-70, 72, 74
    limitations in solving homelessness, 3, 4, 65
progressive change
    limitations of top-down approach, 3-4
    role of protest in creating. *See* protest
protest
    as a means for creating change, 2, 4, 63-65
    disruption as an effective form of, 55-56, 58-59, 72, 75
    rioting as a form of, 52
    See also social movements
protest movements. *See* social movements

Q

Quayle, Dan, 68

R

racism, 69, 76
Reagan, Ronald, 17, 18, 19, 20, 21, 22, 23, 24, 27, 34, 64
recession, 13, 24
redistribution of wealth, 7-8, 17-26. *See also* economic disparity
redlining. *See* housing
relative deprivation, 31
research on homelessness. *See* homelessness
Resource Mobilization Theory, 52
rich and poor. *See* economic disparity
rioting. *See* protest
Roosevelt, Franklin, 2, 49, 63, 65

S

Savings and Loan bailout, 19
service employment. *See* jobs
shanty settlements, 34, 51
Smith, Felida, 74
Smith, Leona, 29, 73
social class structure, 1, 3, 4, 7-8, 12-14, 26, 27, 32, 33, 35, 42, 46,
    47, 48, 50-51
social movements
    consciousness-raising in, 28, 30, 32, 46-49
    coordinated actions in, 52-55, 57, 75
    development of solidarity in, 52-55, 61, 71, 75
    emergence of, 3, 30-33, 50
    public support of, 56-58
    repression of, 56, 57, 76
    resources for, 52-53, 56, 61
    spontaneous actions in, 52-53, 57
    violence in, 57-58, 75-76
    See also protest
Sprowal, Chris, 29, 68
substance abuse, 1, 26-27, 28, 66
supply-side economics, 21

T

takeovers, corporate. *See* corporations
tax policy
    1981 Economic Recovery Act, 20
    1986 Tax Reform Act, 20, 21
    changes under Reagan, 18, 20-21
    Clinton's proposals to change. *See* Clinton
tent cities, 30, 34, 51, 55, 58, 59
Third World countries, 9-10, 43, 61
tight money supply, 18, 21-22, 37-38
top-down change. *See* progressive change
"trickle down" economics, 21, 33

U

unemployment, 13-14, 31, 32, 37, 41, 44, 45
Unemployment Insurance Benefits, 24
unions, labor. *See* labor unions
Unions of the Homeless, 2, 3, 4, 29, 55, 58, 68, 72, 79
    national headquarters. *See* National Union of the
        Homeless
Up and Out of Poverty Now, 2, 4, 29, 30, 55, 58, 68, 72, 79
uprisings. *See* protest

V

veterans among homeless. *See* homelessness, characteristics of
    victims
victim blaming
    as response to homelessness, 1, 4, 26-28
    government's role in, 26-28
    media's role in, 27
    researchers role in, 26-27, 66
voting patterns. *See* electoral patterns

W

wages, jobs. *See* jobs
welfare reform, 40-41
Welfare Rights Organization, 29
Welfare Rights Unions, 2, 4, 29, 55, 58, 72, 79
women among homeless. *See* homelessness, characteristics of
    victims
Women, Infants and Children (WIC), 39-40
Women's Movement, 75